BEYOND ORDER MAKERS

Target Marketing, Branding, and Business Development for Entrepreneurs

By

Alison L. Mullins

Published by Rep Methods LLC

BEYOND ORDER MAKERS

Target Marketing, Branding, and Business Development for Entrepreneurs

© Copyright 2024 – Alison L. Mullins

All rights reserved. The content contained within this book may not be reproduced, duplicated or transmitted without direct written permission from the author or the publisher.

Published by Rep Methods LLC

Paperback ISBN	978-0-9601287-0-9
E-Book ISBN	978-0-9601287-1-6
Hardcover ISBN	978-0-9601287-2-3

Under no circumstances will any blame or legal responsibility be held against the publisher, or author, for any damages, reparation, or monetary loss due to the information contained within this book, either directly or indirectly.

Legal Notice:

This book is copyright protected. It is only for personal use. You cannot amend, distribute, sell, use, quote or paraphrase any part, or the content within this book, without the consent of the author or publisher.

Disclaimer Notice:

Please note the information contained within this document is for educational and entertainment purposes only. All effort has been executed to present accurate, up to date, reliable, complete information. No warranties of any kind are declared or implied. Readers acknowledge that the author is not engaged in the rendering of legal, financial, medical or professional advice.

By reading this document, the reader agrees that under no circumstances is the author responsible for any losses, direct or indirect, that are incurred as a result of the use of the information contained within this document, including, but not limited to, errors, omissions, or inaccuracies.

My heartfelt thanks to everyone who has supported me on this journey, both personally and professionally.

*Keep dreaming, keep climbing, never settle and
never sit in the back row.*

Breathe, by Becky Helmsley

*She sat at the back, and they said she was shy,
She led from the front, and they hated her pride,
They asked her advice and then questioned her guidance,
They branded her loud, then were shocked by her silence,*

*When she shared no ambition, they said it was sad,
So, she told them her dreams and they said she was mad,
They told her they'd listen, then covered their ears,
And gave her a hug while they laughed at her fears,*

*And she listened to all of it thinking she should,
Be the girl they told her to be best as she could,
But one day she asked what was best for herself,
Instead of trying to please everyone else,
So, she walked to the forest and stood with the trees,*

*She heard the wind whisper and dance with the leaves,
She spoke to the willow, the elm and the pine,
And she told them what she'd been told time after time,
She told them she was never enough,
She was either too little or far too much,*

*Too loud or too quiet, too fierce or too weak,
Too wise or too foolish, too bold or too meek,
Then she found a small clearing surrounded by firs,
And she stopped...and she heard what the trees said to her,
And she sat there for hours not wanting to leave,
For the forest said nothing, it just let her breathe.* [1]

---

[1] Becky Hemsley, *Breathe* (Beverley, UK: Mudlark and Sparrow, 2021).

TABLE OF CONTENTS

Foreword — 1

Preface — 5

SECTION 1 - Mastering the Art of Branding — 9
Crafting an Indirect Selling Technique

CHAPTER 1: Foundational Brand Elements — 11
Target Persona & Unique Value Propositions

CHAPTER 2: Mastering the Art of Brand Strategy — 23
Constructing a Strategic Marketing Blueprint

CHAPTER 3: Developing a Visual Identity — 37
Harnessing the Influence of Visuals in Branding

CHAPTER 4: Building Bonds Through Brand Architecture — 49
Techniques for Engaging Clients and Selling with Attraction

SECTION 2 - Mastering Target Marketing — 79
Unlocking Business Development

CHAPTER 5: Beyond the Octopus — 81
Target Marketing and Prioritization

CHAPTER 6: Mastering Engagement — 121
Rethink Business Relationships & Attraction Selling

CHAPTER 7: Training and Professional Development
for Targeted Business Growth   147

CHAPTER 8: Embracing Technology,
Rethinking Leverage   157

SECTION 3 - Mastering Target the Human Element   179
A Psychological and Operational Aspect of Sales

CHAPTER 9: The Human Element   181
Emotional Intelligence and Selling

CHAPTER 10: The Human Element   207
Buyer Psychology

CHAPTER 11: Humanizing Mentality   225
A Work-Life Balance Conversation

CHAPTER 12: Humanizing Tasks   243
Time-Management Skills to Maximize Operational Success

CHAPTER 13: Manifestation Selling   275
A New Perspective on Setting and Achieving Sales Goals

Final Remarks   291
Index   293
About The Author   305

FOREWORD

By Bill Soroka

Chief Dot Connector and founder, NotaryCoach.com

Every single one of us is in sales. I know, I know—some of you just cringed. I resisted this concept for most of my professional life too. The word "sales" often conjures up images of overenthusiastic, fast-talking, salespeople desperate to close the deal. But selling, true selling, isn't about pushy pitches; it's about connection, communication, and understanding what people need—even if they don't know they need or want it yet.

You see, whether you're a notary (like my tribe), an entrepreneur, a teacher, or even a parent, you are selling something. It could be your skills, your ideas, or even the notion that yes, your child really does need to eat their veggies or brush their teeth.

Sales is woven into the fabric of our everyday interactions. And if we can reframe it from this daunting, uncomfortable act to a skillset that opens doors, inspires trust, and solves problems, well, suddenly the world starts to look a lot more exciting. As a business owner, or salesperson, this is how you bring value to your customer relationships. And one of the great lessons I've learned in my career is that you truly are compensated in direct proportion to the value you bring to the marketplace.

Foreword

That's where this book comes in. Alison, clearly a master of sales and branding, gets it. She knows that the secret to selling isn't in bombarding people with endless facts and figures, but in crafting an irresistible story around your brand. It's about showing up authentically, understanding your target audience, and making them feel heard, seen, and valued.

What I love about this book is that it doesn't just hand you a sales script and wish you luck (I've read plenty of those kinds of books). Instead, it walks you through the art of branding—the unsung hero of successful sales, often forgotten or deprioritized as we're busy bootstrapping our business or career. Imagine trying to sell a product or service without a clear, compelling brand. You'd be like a ship lost at sea, without a rudder. Oh, you'll get somewhere all right, but not likely where you want or when. But with a solid brand identity, you know exactly where you're going, and so do your customers.

Alison breaks down the process of building that brand, piece by piece, in a way that is both approachable and insightful. I can't tell you how many "aha!" moments I had while reading this. Concepts that once seemed nebulous suddenly made sense, all thanks to the clear explanations, real-world examples, and her knowledge frameworks presented here.

The brilliance of this book lies in its recognition of the human element in sales. This isn't just about sealing the deal, it's about fostering genuine relationships, building trust, and yes, telling a story that resonates. As you read Beyond Order Makers today, you'll realize that salespeople aren't just order takers; they're relationship makers. And if you can master that, you can build a book of business in any industry.

In today's digital age, when communication is often reduced to screens and swipes, the ability to connect authentically is more valuable than ever. This book's emphasis on empathy, active listening, and crafting meaningful interactions is a breath of fresh air. Whether you're selling a physical product, a service, or even just an idea, understanding the psychology behind human connection is key. Don't worry, you don't need a Ph.D. in psychology to understand consumer behavior. Alison teaches it with ease and finesse.

Here's the thing: no matter what field you're in, you're going to find yourself in a position where you need to influence, persuade, or connect with someone. You'll need to articulate why your product, service, or even your idea is the solution someone's been looking for. And if you can master that skill, you can open doors to countless opportunities.

I've built my career on connecting with people, sharing stories, and helping others do the same. And I can tell you, this book is packed with practical advice, thoughtful insights, and step-by-step guides that will not only make you a better seller but a more effective communicator. It's not about being slick; it's about being real. It's about understanding your audience, knowing your brand, and showing up as the best version of yourself.

Reading this book felt like having a conversation with a friend who genuinely wants to see you succeed. And, because I know Alison, I know that to be exactly true. Her approach to sales and branding is refreshing, and these insights she shares here are exactly what today's entrepreneurs need. It's less about traditional sales tactics and more about creating authentic, lasting connections—and that's a message I can get behind.

PREFACE

Whatever vision has brought you to the business world, I have designed this book to help you work smarter, not harder. Specifically tailored for small business owners and entrepreneurs, this book provides valuable insights and strategies to "reset your sales settings." I cover the tools and resources necessary for success, from branding to selling, target marketing to the psychology of sales.

Everyone is in sales. Period.

At some point, you have sold something. It could be selling yourself in a job interview or persuading a bank to approve a home loan. Maybe you're a wedding planner, painting visual dreams with words for a bride and groom. A travel agent depicting *the* dream vacation as a seamless package. At some point, has selling become an obstacle?

Many an entrepreneur starts with a dream to own a business, but most can't imagine having to sell to be successful. For example, creatives who loathe public attention, wishing they could remove the responsibilities of selling to another. Or the woman with a bright vision to bring natural products to the market, but her passion is for nature, not business. How about a young person with immense talent for writing code, but zero skills in the people department.

Now, imagine that fear fading away. Imagine your business's selling process and development portion becoming easier, smoother, and more effective with a firmer grasp of branding, target marketing and standard methodical & operational changes.

What if I could help you relieve that anxiety and generate confidence to move past the fear, find new business, and start selling? Smarter, not harder.

What if, instead of relying on the ordinary solutions found in fat business books, all it requires is a brief examination of branding and sales strategies and, most challenging of all, assessing one's own human character requirements for success?

Imagine creating a more effective brand strategy, transforming sales goals into manageable fragments, and watching your business thrive. Imagine improving your target marketing plan by eliminating the ineffective "throwing the spaghetti at the wall" approach. Imagine buying back the time wasted on advertising to the wrong client, pitching the wrong board, or attending a networking group that will bring zero ROI.

The Power of this Book

You can have it all. This book offers you valuable tools to navigate this journey with the assurance that I am here to support you, answer questions, and guide you with every step.

Expansion and Transformation

Over the last few years, I've collected feedback from customers and audiences, shaping this book into an expansion guide based on the most requested topics. The response to my first book was so incredible that I felt compelled to write another, linking the innovative marketing techniques that have helped me as an entrepreneur.

This book will

- give you insights and real-life, down-and-dirty techniques that will transform your business's selling dynamics forever
- teach you how to use data more effectively, streamline work processes, and apply branding and target marketing tactics
- help you break down massive sales goals into manageable pieces and manifest productivity

Above all, this book will change not only how you think about selling but give you a roadmap of exactly where and how to go get those sales.

Acknowledgment of Artificial Intelligence (AI) Tools

I want to recognize and clarify how I used AI tools for this book. Advanced technologies like ChatGPT, an AI language model, helped expand my outlines. DALL·E, an AI image creation tool by OpenAI, helped me customize and translate my subject visions into images, which improved this book's visual content. Given the limitations of AI image creation tools, you may notice a few spelling errors on images where AI translated the image from my mind, into a graphic. I've left many of these images in their original format and left the sometimes-eerie misspellings by choice.

The power of AI has been an amazing tool for me not only rounding out challenges in drafting this book, but also in my

Preface

day-to-day efforts to continuously craft custom messages for my audience. The art of translating what comes in and out of my brain into something that can teach others is no simple task. I collaborated with a professional editor and proofreader to ensure high-quality content. I could not do this alone.

SECTION 1

Mastering the Art of Branding

Crafting an Indirect Selling Technique

CHAPTER 1
Foundational Brand Elements
Target Persona & Unique Value Propositions

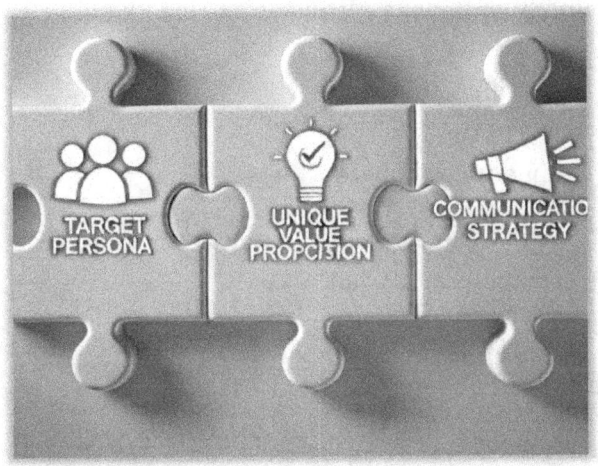

Better Target Marketing = Better Business Development = More Sales

The strategic importance of a well-defined brand is a key player in the intricate dance of business development and target marketing. A robust and consistent brand is the cornerstone of effective target marketing. When your brand's messaging and values perfectly harmonize with your UVP, they resonate more deeply with your target persona. This alignment ensures that every communication, campaign, and customer interaction reinforce the distinctive attributes and benefits that set your business apart. Such consistency increases brand recognition and trust, enhancing marketing campaign effectiveness by focusing on attracting and keeping the ideal customer base. This important step will also define how you formulate each sales pitch.

Foundations for branding include several elements:

- structured target persona
- unique value proposition (UVP) statement or statements
- communication strategy
- point of view
- competitive analysis

(To make this easier to read, from now on, I'll refer to unique value propositions as UVPs.)

In this chapter we are going to explore how to formulate two of the most difficult to conceive: **UVP & Target Persona**.

I personally suggest starting to develop these two items first, save the brand strategy for after you've perfected these two things.

When I started Rep Methods, I often flipped back and forth to develop my target persona. I had the UVP (or so I thought). Like me, you'll flip back and forth between them and adjust accordingly. The most important concept to consider is that these pillars are underlying derivatives of each other. They feed off one another, and tweaking one can alter the others. Confused? Don't be. We'll talk about each of these pillars in depth in a moment.

A well-defined brand acts as a beacon, simplifying the decision-making process for potential clients. It creates a clear expectation of what your company represents and promises, reducing the cognitive load on customers when choosing your products or services over competitors. This clarity is crucial and comforting in business development, as it helps streamline lead qualification, enhances customer acquisition strategies, and improves conversion rates, providing a sense of reassurance and ease.

Brand equity plays a pivotal role. Brand equity refers to the value and strength of a brand that determines its worth. High brand equity means customers perceive your brand as high quality and reliable, which can justify premium pricing and foster strong customer loyalty. Investing in building and maintaining brand equity ensures that your brand remains a trusted choice for consumers, further enhancing your business development efforts.

To invest in brand equity, you want to ensure your brand consistently reflects your **UVP** and addresses the needs and preferences of your **target persona**.

By communicating effectively through our brand, we build relationships. Strong relationships are established through understanding and trust, cultivating loyalty, and driving repeat business. In this way, your brand becomes a powerful tool for marketing and comprehensive business development, helping pave the way for sustainable growth and success. It's become clear to me over the years, the relationships I develop are how I sell. One theme you will also find prevalent throughout this book: **It's easier to sell when we approach the right customers.**

Aligning your brand with your UVP is not just a strategy; it's like bringing two continents together, forming a cohesive pathway toward consistent messaging. Once solidified, your UVP reinforces your brand's identity and communicates why your brand exists. Having this backbone, you can now work on your sales pitch, target markets, communication strategy, and, of course, visual identity. By doing so, you develop the power to shape a narrative and create an appealing argument for the target audience about why they should buy from you.

While on this journey of discovery, ponder a couple of questions as you move along:

- What **value** do you place on the products or services you offer?
- Who are you **guaranteed** to attract?
- Who do you **want** to attract?
- How is your business or your products **different** from what's already on the shelves?

Target Persona

Discovering the core target persona begins with identifying the vision of a primary customer. Remember, you can come back anytime and tweak any part of these foundational components. Let's get started!

The target persona is one person, character, and tiny player by which you will create all brand elements.

When my brand coach first asked me to create a target persona, I began with who I thought my customer was supposed to be, but to my surprise, I was utterly wrong about who my customer would become.

My coaches reeled me in several times because I kept attempting to broaden this customer into an industry, a group, a category! I really wanted to create a "broad spectrum" client group that was very industry specific. Yet they kept reminding me to focus on the singular entity. Oddly enough, by intentionally focusing on a smaller scope, we can attract a broader range of clients in the future since our narrowed design tactics help establish our brand and strengthen our sales pitch overall.

I was amazed to find out that the ideal person was aligned with who I am as a person. My intended audience is actually a woman just like me, the group, the industry has nothing to do with it.

To get to the core of who we are selling to, we must identify this singular person, defining their core environments. Typically, when a professional marketer thinks about target marketing, they tend to focus on the fundamental demographics we learn in school or through our experiences in business: zip codes, age, race, and monetary status. But when working on a sales pitch, formulating a brand strategy—or, in my case, defining why I was coming to market with a new business model—you need to learn how psychographics come into play far beyond the age-old demographics.

(Remember, I have an entire section devoted to target markets and the prioritization of customers that will help you expand your brand's reach. So, this is just the overview.)

I'd been taught to consider one individual, believing others "will come." Without getting too much into my "field of dreams" mentality, that's where we are: "If you build it, they will come." Start with one personality and don't worry about the rest of the customers who will come.

Here are a few questions to get you started. Write down the answers to help you begin to identify this real human character. Don't worry, you'll have room to make changes later.

- ☐ What does a day in life look like for the person who buys your products or services?
- ☐ Where do they go after work?
- ☐ What do they do on the weekends?
- ☐ Do they have a family or prefer a single life?
- ☐ Are they religious?
- ☐ What do they typically eat at home?
- ☐ Where do they go to eat out with friends or family?
- ☐ What do they pick up to read?
- ☐ Where do they shop for clothes?
- ☐ Do they wear a specific brand of apparel?
- ☐ Where do they buy their groceries?
- ☐ What color would you find on the walls in their kitchen?
- ☐ What is their favorite fragrance?

It may seem odd to go into such personal details. As an entrepreneur, it's often easier to begin visualizing the brand concepts such as logo, color schemes and maybe even a catchphrase. However, without digging deep into the considerations of who will actually buy the products, how do we know our design is the right fit? It's reminiscent of another old adage, "putting the cart before the horse."

Our focus is on selling to someone who needs a solution, not necessarily selling to ourselves. Placing yourself in your consumer's shoes helps us start on a better footing. Remember, you aren't limiting your offerings to one entity by creating one persona. Instead, you're creating a voice that echoes across your media, merchandising, and marketing and even aligns your network with other businesses.

Unique Value Propositions

It's one thing to have a unique idea for entrepreneurship. It's another challenge to find buyers who will embrace this idea. Selling anything requires making a statement, or group of statements that will hold value in the minds of prospective buyers. This statement(s) is the UVP—it's not just a statement; it's the tool needed to attract customers to a product. Looking back to the target persona, this UVP statement or group of statements should touch on the points of uncertainty or identify the needs within our target persona. Once we have a general draft for our UVP, it becomes easier to round out a brand strategy. We can then create a content strategy and further define both aspects of the target persona and the UVP. It's also worth noting that aspects of your UVP will eventually become part of your detailed sales pitch(es). If we begin to do this work now, it will make selling much easier later.

Yes, the UVP can help you go back and further define the target persona, as I mentioned it's the "chicken and the egg." Working on these statements requires a healthy back-and-forth balance between these two core elements. When it's working correctly, you will feel satisfied as your idea, service, product, or brand starts to form. Keep in mind that you may face challenges during the development process. Also, watch out for scalability. This year, I struggled with overcoming the reality that my target persona for this book needed to match the intended target persona laid out in my original business plan. As I developed a new brand strategy for *Beyond Order Makers*, it actually began to help me redefine the target persona and clarify the details of my business Rep Methods. My coaches reminded me to keep the focus on my persona and UVP based on personality characteristics, key demographics, and problems that needed solving, where my business model could be the solution. As our businesses grow, we might add products or services, so we need to keep those generalized within these pillar elements and leave the specifics out of it. For instance, I may offer boot camps, but the UVP doesn't need to outline the length of time, cost, or any other details or contain a broad description of the customizable option. Make sense? Keep name brands, products, and specifics out of your UVP. Keep the focus on the solutions you provide.

Rep Methods UVP story

While drafting my first attempt at a UVP, I began with a motto I developed for the first book published in 2023 called *The Art of Selling, We Make Order Makers, Not Order Takers*. The motto "We Make Order Makers, Not Order Takers" is now trademarked and is the defining element behind my sales training mentality. That's the separation from other sales training methodologies. It's proactive, not reactive. It's straightforward. It's reliable and shows a follow-through, follow-up, and forward-moving mentality. The strength in those few words is the defining motivation for the company's existence. To my disbelief, when I submitted this to my brand coach, I was told it wasn't a UVP but an excellent start! My coaches said, "No, try again." "Be more thoughtful," they said. "Be more inclusive" and "Tell us whom you serve." My ego was crushed, of course, but I went to work tweaking statements and sending drafts via Loomly over to the strategy team. Ultimately, I'm glad I did the job and didn't hire out because it gave me this understanding of moving back and forth between developing the persona and the statements. I was surprised to learn the result would be a conglomerate of sentences and more "statements" than expected. Initially, I looked at the UVP as my tagline, and while the tagline or motto is essential, it's not the defining statement of my business. It's a small portion of a whole. My coaching team worked tirelessly to help me get to the final UVP. So, without further ado, here is the final approved brand strategy UVP for Rep Methods.

Rep Methods is in the transformation business.

We Make Order Makers, Not Order Takers

Rep Methods is a sales training company that caters to entrepreneurs and small businesses that cannot hire a dedicated sales manager, providing them with services and educational opportunities.

Designed with salespeople in mind, Rep Methods training programs focus on improving skills such as time management, organization, prioritization, and follow-up. By honing these specific skills, sales professionals can shift from reactive to proactive selling.

> The initiative, nurturing, honesty, thoughtfulness, and follow-through are all qualities that Rep Methods training cultivates, making our clients responsible, successful, and remarkable salespeople.
>
> Rep Methods offers a range of options for individuals, including seminars, workshops, coaching programs, bootcamps, and online programming.

Take a few minutes and start crafting a few statements about the brand you sell, the service you provide, or your recently formed business. Play with the thoughts and words and consider the target persona identified earlier.

Having formed your first go at a target persona and UVP, you're ready with the foundations for a real-life brand strategy. Once in place, you can create a point of view! Your understanding of your ideal client has reached a point where you can even describe their food preferences for Friday nights. You know what colors will resonate with them. You can hear how they sound, and you know their needs intuitively. Above all, you know exactly why you created this business or took this sales position and how you will craft your presence in the marketplace.

BEYOND ORDER MAKERS

CHAPTER 2

Mastering the Art of Brand Strategy

Constructing a Strategic Marketing Blueprint

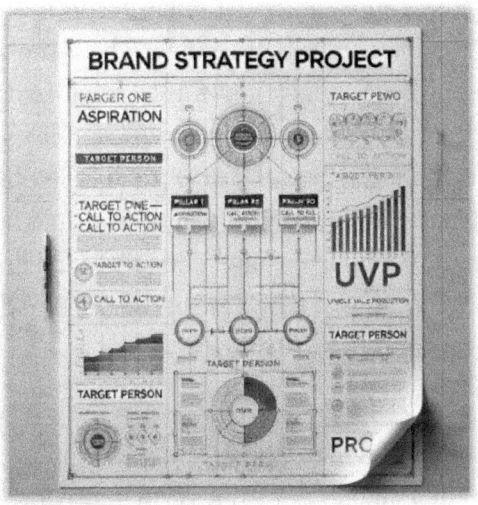

After completing the **UVP & Target Persona** discussed in the previous chapter, crafting a communication strategy is the next step for small businesses and entrepreneurs who eventually hope to hand off advertising, marketing, or media subcontractors to lighten our heavy entrepreneurial loads. New business owners have the hardest time balancing all the duties required to be successful. With this process, you will be ready to take one thing off your plate and confidently place it in the hands of someone else to help you along the way.

Chapter 2

Creating a Communication Strategy

What's the first thing you think of in terms of a "brand"? It's the logo, but is it the name? Before we discuss the visual ties that bind, we must tell the consumer a story. Think about our ancestors. Ancient ancestors drew story visuals on cave walls, communicated stories to pass down knowledge, shared experiences, and helped make sense of the developing world around them. Fast forward to today, and those visual stories are just as powerful. In sales, storytelling is like waving a wand. It's not about listing facts and features; it's about painting a picture and creating an experience. When we hear about the story behind the purchase, it's no longer just a thing that happened. It's a symbol, a dream, an ingrained part of our lives. That's the secret sauce of a killer brand story. It's not just about selling; it's about striking a chord with people and making them feel something real. We build a vision and create the dream in their brains once we've shown the value of the thing in the story. It's like building a friendship—solid, dependable, and here for the long haul.

The story is like winter tire chains, or the chalk rock climbers use to keep their hands dry on a vertical ascent. The story is there, while often not highly noticeable. Its purpose is to bring strength, validity, and traction to our place in the market. Storytelling forms the foundation of a brand's identity and connects to our consumers on a deeper level. Crafting an exciting brand story goes beyond just conveying information; it evokes emotions, builds trust, and fosters long-lasting customer relationships.

For salespeople and companies, telling the story is easy. What about a smoothie shop? The images of health, fruits, vegetables, anti-stress, new age, beauty, and brightness come across in the imagery. If we own a countertop fabrication shop, we show the latest technology and a wide selection of materials while showcasing the ease of process and procedure. We may be interior designers, where showcasing the work we've executed becomes prevalent to the client we want to get, or an artist whose work must convey a direct message to the heart of the target buyer.

The story comes through in the presentation. When walking into a retail store, restaurant, or showroom, you must consider the feeling that arrives once you cross the threshold. Does the environment suit you? Consider how you feel when entering a children's toy store. For me, it's overwhelming because I don't have children, and I don't know where to begin my search for the gift I'm considering for purchase. But then I am not their target persona.

Marketing and advertising are all adept at recruiting customers through our doors, and it starts with a brand story and communication strategy. Kind of like our brand strategy, a communication strategy has three pillars as well! The target market is the aspirational appeal, the UVP is the call to action, and the communication strategy is the proof of how we show our potential customers our solutions work.

The Role of Storytelling in Sales

Telling stories is vital in enabling clients to appreciate the profound influences of nature, innovative visions previously unrecognized, and gain the exclusivity of purchasing from a visionary leader in the industry. I'm going to show you a couple of examples of luxury brands strategic ability in storytelling, combined with consistent visual identity. The vision conveyed through these stories not only sells the products but also builds the brand's aspirational foundation. It's a cycle where storytelling, visualization, and brand alignment converge to drive sales, with each element reinforcing the others, creating a brand that is both a legend and a benchmark in the industry.

In the following case studies, I want to show you how storytelling applies to the communication strategy for a brand. Let's look at these three masters of storytelling in branding.

Case study: Ralph Lauren

Every seasonal apparel, luggage, home, or accessory collection starts with a story, a vision board. Each quarter a new vision board begins deep in the rooms of the Madison Avenue design house with a legendary workspace designed to elevate and capture the hearts and minds of employees, reminding us every day where we work and how the brand began. When we walked through the doors, Ralph and the team instilled the value of equestrian clubs, sports, and social clubs from floor to ceiling. Each season was designed with a destination in mind or a specialty time or event. Each season, we were presented with a collection exuding elegance, refinement, luxury, and quintessential equestrian roots. The foundation is within the undertone of every advertisement—aspirational desire, calling customers to belong. The proof is in the happiness and contentment highlighted in each photograph. The new-to-market pieces hold value and a purpose for the future owner. Each garment fits a vision based on destination or purpose. The stories conveyed provide purpose and necessity.

Think, "Why must I have the new cotton polo cardigan set for my trip? It's Sint Marteen, and I must fit in while traveling to this exclusive resort." Perhaps it's the man purchasing a new parka stocked this fall and emulating the Prince of Wales stalking game in Scotland that meets the emotional need of a certain 30–50 plus American male. Boards highlighting luxury ski trips in Vail, Colorado, or Switzerland are building the dream for the new RLX puffer coat to be designed for winter. The vision and the stories invite the designers and even consumers to be "a part of" and slowly, over time, build a Fortune 500 brand sustaining the test of time in American consumerism.

Case study: Antolini, Italy

Creating a branded natural product. I.E. this company manufacturers and transforms natural materials sourced directly from the earth is a challenge. Antolini, Italy has risen to this challenge for over thirty years while setting standards in branding natural stone within the industry, where typically no single entity controls the entire process—from quarry to customer. Like the coal industry, which involves multiple stakeholders (from landowners to shippers), the natural stone business is similarly fragmented. Yet, Antolini has managed to carve out a unique and powerful niche, visually showcasing their brand to exemplify the highest quality of stone available for purchase.

When I joined this industry giant, I quickly fell in love with the narratives embedded in each piece of stone. These stories were crucial in securing sales through specifications with top architects and designers. Understanding the origins of the quarries and the extensive efforts the company invested in each piece of stone significantly boosted our sales efficacy.

Chapter 2

One fascinating story that enhanced the brand's market position is the exclusive marble variety, Bianco Lasa Covelano Macchia Vecchia. Nestled in northern Italy, the quarry is split between two families from the Laas and Covelano regions. Despite common misconceptions, these families don't necessarily own the land but lease it, a common practice in Italy reminiscent of land leasing in the US coal industry. This quarry produces exquisite white marble veined with grey and gold—the whitest blocks destined for sculptures, while those with gold veins are perfect for luxurious bathrooms and flooring.

The transformation of one marble variety of "trash" to treasure illustrates the power of vision and storytelling in branding. Discarded initially because of its black amphibolite veins, which were thought to devalue the otherwise pristine marble, Mr. Antolini saw potential where others saw imperfection. Experimenting with these blocks created stunning river-like marble staircases, first as an experiment and later as a sought-after design element. This innovation was displayed across the US, capturing designers' imaginations and setting a new trend in luxury marble use.

Try to notice how each of these brands uses a visual and a story to sell without having to have a specific sales pitch? Antolini and Ralph Lauren don't need to actively seek new customers, customers come to them! Their brand story and minimalist marketing approach create reach. Selling without having to sell.

In chapter four you will find a case study which provides both a collaboration of storytelling sales, and it segways the formation of an informal sales tactic through establishing a community voice in collaboration with another brand. In that chapter I show you an example of an interview and collaboration of branding between my company and the AI startup Deep Reel[2] I chose to keep this later in chapter four during the *establishing a brand community section* of the book. Feel free to jump there now if you wish before we move on to more about creating communication strategy.

Professional marketers such as my 2023 marketing coach, Strong Brand Social, led by Katie Wight[3] have helped me to work out these amazing strategies I'm passing along to you today. Marketers refer to three pillars of reach, combined with our target persona, UVP, point of view and competitive analysis as a "brand playbook"—kind of like the football coach has his binder of magic tricks ready to pull out a play whenever a specific goal is presented during the game. Our communication strategy becomes our playbook for the brand. We want to use the three pillars in various combinations across all marketing mediums to plan how we will communicate to our audience and keep the story going.

Pillar One–Aspiration

---

[2] Beta.deepreel.com
[3] Katie Wight, owner and leader of Strong Brand Social, *Strong Brand Social*, accessed September 1, 2023, https://strongbrandsocial.com/.

Chapter 2

Pillar Two–Call to Action

Pillar Three–Proof

When we tap into the values, beliefs, aspirations, problems, and needs of our consumers, we can create a narrative that resonates with them personally. This narrative, I believe, will solidify brand loyalty and all the benefits that come with that loyalty. Storytelling creates an emotional connection, setting our brand apart and making us memorable in a crowded marketplace.

Launching a business can be challenging, especially with the increasing demand for visually appealing content on social media and online platforms, making it overwhelming for many independent entrepreneurs. But you've made it this far; you

BEYOND ORDER MAKERS

are almost there and almost ready to create a brand strategy or content strategy to help take your selling to the next level.

To get started creating a successful communication strategy, let's take a moment and answer more detailed questions about your customer and see what comes to fruition.

What are your clients' essential characteristics?

- Who do they look like? Is there an actor you can use as an example?
- What are their demographics such as male, female, age range, style?
- Can you name a clothing brand to describe them?
- What do they mean to you? How does this client make you feel when they walk in the door or if you get an email inquiry from this client?
- Why do you want their business?
- What nationality is this client?
- What gender is this client?
- Does this client have a family/kids?

- What does this client do on a Friday night?
- Where does this person eat out? Chain or local?
- Who is your direct competitor? Name two companies, local or national.
- What business do you aspire to be like?
- Do you have a "mentor" business?
- What is your company's UVP?
- What 5–10 sentences explain what you do that differentiates your product or service from the competition?
- How do you want your brand to be perceived in the market?
- What ONE statement would you use to describe your business?
- What's your favorite visual representation of your business right now on social media?
- What is your primary business goal on social media?
  - Community Engagement
  - Lead Generation
  - Online Transactions/Sales
- What are your communication goals?
- What do you want from your customers?

Now that you've answered the questions, go back to the target persona story. What would you change? What might you add? What about your UVP? See how they are related, like a little brand description family.

Now I want you to start putting all these items together in a sharable document like Word, Excel, or Google Doc, OK? Go ahead and make a page for that target persona, then throw in those UVP statements on a separate page. Take your notes and start crafting a brand story and maybe you'll even start to feel the brand voice coming through the pages. Next, create a page for your communication strategies including each pillar: 1) Aspirational, 2) Call to action, 3) Proof

Next, I want you to scour the internet for images that meet your expectations for communicating each pillar. Place them on each page like a collage!

Next, I want you to create a blank page to copy and paste visuals representing both what you imagine would help translate the brand to the audience and what you wouldn't recommend a marketer or creative use to describe the points from the UVP. As an entrepreneur, the feelings that develop on things that don't fit our brand are often easier to identify than imagery that does! I'll also note this is challenging because we don't know what is going to resonate with our customers; we simply know the brand aesthetics we've created thus far and we don't have a lot of "proof," so I simply ask you do the best you can to find some visuals that represent your customer and brand.

Put it all together. Looking back, look at what you've created thus far. A real workbook all about your company and brand and you've managed to identify what it will look like and what it absolutely should not look like to the outside world. Go ahead, give yourself a pat on the back.

Next, let's pull in the storytelling aspect. Make up a story about this target persona, situations happening in their lives that cause them to pick up the phone or visit your website and start to peruse your products or services. Play that tape through and write everything about their shopping, quoting, purchasing, and feedback experience. Now you've set the tone for exactly what transactions with your business will look and feel like in real life, or at least how we want them to occur.

Finally, think about your developing "playbook" and what quarters or months of the year might be important transactional periods, and let's start to consider a calendar-based plan on how we might tweak, strengthen, lighten up our advertising or marketing output to meet those expectations.

Ask yourself the following questions:

- What time of year do I expect to make the most sales?
- Is this seasonal and if so, what's the next best time I would expect to have the most customers?
- Based on my target persona, where would my customers most likely see, hear, or scroll through visuals?
- What times of day are my shoppers engaging with online social media?
- When do my shoppers read their emails?
- What radio stations do my shoppers listen to?

I want you to go back to that target persona document and add the answers to these questions. You are now ready to pull it all together and identify what, when, how, and how often your business needs to be using marketing and media outlets!

Congratulations, you've created a brand handbook that is ready to share, turnover, or be discussed with any media professional. Whew, what a relief!

Think about it for just a moment: with all this information outlined, you will be prepared for any of the following situations likely to occur when owning a business:

- interact with a radio salesperson competing for the best advertising time and stations
- creating ads for social media yourself or using a subcontractor
- placing paid ads on Google or social media
- buying television advertising space
- hiring actors to play roles in recorded ads
- deciding which product or service needs to be highlighted in all media placement
- sending marketing emails to clients
- posting content on social media
- creating social media content
- when to offer promotional discounts
- when to tighten the budgets for marketing and hold down the fort

Of course, there is always room for more detailed analysis like the ever-evolving questions we see in marketers advertising their services:

- Aren't I supposed to post every day?
- How many times should I post a video during the week?
- How many TikTok's vs Facebook reels?
- Should I change my content for LinkedIn?

These are just a few example queries where marketing amateurs are trying to read the algorithms of the social media giants and predict what will "reach." I'm here to tell you to stop trying to figure it out and simply make your own playbook based on your target persona and your UVPs. The rest will fall into place as you see the returns on the efforts you are putting into placing customized content in the areas defined by your customer base. Enough with the "I need eighteen hashtags" if

Chapter 2

I want to get seen. Just follow what works for your clients and forget about the rest. Now some critics might argue that not using some of the social nuances with visual content is a no-no, so I say yes, identify the hashtags that go with your business and use them every time, but there is no sense in trying to define what and how many because the powerhouse social companies change their wish lists too often. Just do you, boo. Enough said.

CHAPTER 3
Developing a Visual Identity
Harnessing the Influence of Visuals in Branding

As we poke around the empire of visual identity in branding design, remember we've already formulated the target persona, laid out a brand story, and are crystal clear on the value we are bringing to the consumers eagerly waiting on the other side.

Now, we're ready to embark on creating a visual identity. Whether we're envisioning a new website, designing a fresh logo, or reevaluating our current brand aesthetics, the role of color is not to be underestimated. Knowing the implications and strategic importance of color choice and aligning it with your branding strategy will ensure that your visual identity supports your business goals and connects meaningfully with your customers.

I recall designing my first logo for Alpha Colores Creative Marketing (now shortened to ACCM). Without researching, I selected colors that felt personal and resonant to me at the time—soft yet dynamic shades of purple and orange. I even included a Hawaiian flower to echo my fascination with volcanoes and floral motifs during a mission to Hawaii in 2017. In hindsight, my approach was driven more by personal preference than by a professional understanding of how colors affect consumer behavior. This experience taught me a valuable lesson: while branding elements must appeal to the creator, they must also align with the expectations and emotions of the target audience.

Let's explore the vibrant world of color in branding. The right palette can not only capture attention but also encapsulate your brand's essence and ethos, paving the way for a stronger connection with your audience.

Importance of Color

Choosing the right colors is particularly important, as they can evoke emotions and ideas and influence consumer perceptions of a brand. By selecting appealing color schemes that align with the persona, UVP, and voice, we can create a visually cohesive and impactful brand identity. I recommend starting with the color wheel to understand what colors balance with each other.

According to two-time best-selling author and tenured marketing vet Anita Nipane, 93 percent of customers make purchase decisions based on color and visual appearance.[4] In her article on digginet.com, she discusses the 60-30-10 rule in graphic design. Every brand should have three colors and use them in proportions of 60, 30, and 10 percent.[5] In the article, she discusses significant brands like McDonalds, Walmart, and DHL. She also discusses how wide-scope offering brands like Microsoft and Google have multicolored logos to insinuate to the consumer the broad scope of their product offerings.

When I began researching the latest sales training company, Rep Methods, my visual branding process started like my old habits from 2016! Luckily, I had gained some years of experience as an LLC while also working and learning the ways of some corporations mentioned above, so I decided to take a deeper look at the colors I would choose and how they would resonate with my target persona before making selections! The original target persona of the business model is *granite stone fabricators needing help teaching salespeople.* These small businesses are known for their hardworking nature, with employees representing various nationalities and ethnicities from all corners of the world. The construction building materials industry we belong to has a disproportionately low representation of female ownership or operation, standing at just 11 percent. Considering this, I consciously focused on creating color combinations that would greatly appeal to male viewers. I could no longer recognize the feminine and hobby tones that characterized my initial business and personal branding experience—they were outdated. The logo and visuals needed to exhibit weight, depth, and a certain level of seriousness to

---

[4] Anita Nipane, "The Power of Color in Marketing," Digginet.com, accessed July 25, 2024, https://www.digginet.com/articles/the-power-of-color-in-marketing.
[5] Anita Nipane, "The Power of Color in Marketing."

Chapter 3

effectively communicate our message. I landed on simple black, bright orange, and white for balance. I chose orange because it emulates "freedom, individuality, originality, optimism, and youth," according to color-meanings.com author Jacob Olesen.[6] Also, according to Olesen, black can evoke negativity such as "death, misfortune, and evil" but also "sleek and chic" or "mysterious and powerful." Black also has an essence of high fashion based on my education at university, and black is the color of sex, "bursting with sex appeal."[7]

In college, while getting a degree in marketing and fashion, we learned that trends begin in Europe and migrate toward the USA. Trends also start with bold, new, and luxury brands before trickling down to the mass market. Take note, color trends are often created years in advance, so it's helpful to research past and future color trends through forecasting agencies such as Pantone, Color Marketing Group, or Coloro. By researching the past, you may make better decisions for the future.

While deciding the colors for Rep Methods, I feel incredibly fortunate to use some of the professional guidelines, but I also followed instincts in making the color selections for the brand. Coincidentally, Pantone, the prestigious organization responsible for color development and with a rich history as the longest-standing color company, has just revealed their selection for Europe's Color of the Year in 2024— a vibrant shade they

---

[6] Jacob Olesen, "Orange Color Symbolism in Literature," Color Meanings, accessed July 25, 2024, https://www.color-meanings.com/orange-color-symbolism-literature/.

[7] Jacob Olesen, "Black Color Meaning–The Color Black," *Color Meanings*, accessed July 25, 2024, https://www.color-meanings.com/black-color-meaning-the-color-black/

have christened "Orange Slice."[8] My timing could not have been more perfect. I got seriously lucky, but I'm especially thankful for the thought process in identifying the persona first, having a motto, and the beginnings of a UVP before making such valuable consumer influentials.

Hopefully, you can feel more prepared with a new perspective on crafting and putting together colors in terms of brand. I notice color elements more than the average person, and I grow bored when I see brands implore stagnant combinations such as "red, white, and blue" (a standard color combo in construction services). Or when I speak with a client with zero concept of what they want from a logo design. It's rather painful when our clients have not done any research before hiring me, and it is even more challenging if they aren't prepared to answer the psychographic and demographic questions in advance.

The Logo

My logo began in a thought process based on the motto, We Make Order Takers, Not Order Makers™; my early UVP involved changing the "settings" of existing and incoming new salespeople. Digging around for icons, I realized the cog wheel we see on all our televisions and digital devices has global recognition for "settings." No matter the language, anyone can find the settings icon to enter the main menu! "Ah-ha," I thought, "that is a successful simplification of my original UVP." The other concept from my business plan was to make the programming simple. I never wanted to complicate the already-complicated world of stone fabrication and wholesale

---

[8] Pantone, "2024 Color of the Year," accessed July 25, 2024, https://www.pantone.com/eu/en/articles/color-of-the-year].

building materials, and I honed in on simplicity. A black background with a simple, bold color name and a third color for balance did the job.

So, you want to start creating this new brand image, the logo, the visual item seen by anyone who interacts with your brand. While many logo generators exist, having the colors defined in your mind, while taking a look back at those visuals we created in the brand strategy, will help you to utilize some of these auto-generating services. One of my all-time favorites is Wix[9]; however, Adobe Express,[10] Canva,[11] and many others offer logo-generating software that mixes the right fonts with the right colors and icons to make suggestions for you! With the work you've already done, it becomes even easier to use any of these predetermining engines to help pull things all together. But for those who want a more tailored and customized approach, I suggest hiring a logo design specialist who will be able to take one look at your brand strategy and start immediately generating ideas on how to make something from scratch for you using from scratch tools like Adobe Illustrator.

These core elements are required to make a logo, so it will be super helpful if you've identified some favorites before contacting a custom designer or starting a logo-generating software program.

- Brand name
- Ideal font(s)
- Tagline

---

[9] https://www.wix.com/logo/maker
[10] https://www.adobe.com/express/create/logo
[11] https://www.canva.com/create/logos/

BEYOND ORDER MAKERS

- Icon or image
- Three colors and the exact shade you prefer. (If you want to go a step further, find out their RGB color numbers for your designer to follow.)

> **Pro Tip!** Are you in love with a specific color? Well, try using an "eye dropper tool" program online to identify that color in its RGB format.

Let's take a look at one brand's use of color and how their brand identity became clear in their visuals and platform for selling.

Chapter 3

> ## Case Study: Schluter-Systems, A Story of Innovation, Visual Identity, and Market Domination

Founded in the 1990s, Schluter-Systems[12] started as a German innovation, primarily known for its revolutionary tools for waterproofing and coatings. Their entry into the US market indicated a pivotal shift in their geographic footprint, branding, and marketing strategy. Recognizing the need to make their products not only functional but visually appealing and memorable, Schluter adopted a bright, distinctive color palette of orange, complemented by grey and white. This choice wasn't just aesthetic but strategic, making their products instantly recognizable and differentiating them within a crowded marketplace.

Visual identity and its affects

The choice of orange—a color often associated with creativity, determination, and success—helped position Schluter as a leader in innovation. This branding strategy was clear in my first encounter with the brand at a CEU seminar hosted by the National Kitchen & Bath Association (NKBA) in Virginia in 2011. As a newcomer to the residential construction industry, I was struck by their presentation's uniformity and visual appeal. The choice of orange for everything—from the product color to the seam seal tape—was about aesthetics and practicality. This bright, eye-catching hue stands out on the shelves and provides a functional benefit, helping contractors easily spot gaps or mistakes during installation. Competitors often used more subdued, less noticeable colors. The fact that Schluter's vibrant,

---

[12] Schluter Systems. Accessed June 25, 2024. https://www.schluter.com/schluter-us/en_US/.

glaringly bright color would eventually be hidden beneath tiles or wall panels did not detract from its utility. Instead, it made Schluter's products extremely memorable and would eventually impart a sense of reliability and quality. Who knew that orange color product could signal to an overseeing general contractor or builder that the contractor was installing the best underlayment possible for their job just by having the signature orange onsite.

The power of storytelling in branding

Throughout the seminar, Schluter's narrative was engaging. They did not just sell a product; they offered a solution—a promise of ease and quality backed by robust German engineering. This approach not only educated potential users but also built a narrative around the brand that spoke directly to the needs and aspirations of its audience. A colleague, Leo Lantz, a tile contractor, demonstrated the impact of this storytelling approach. He saw Schluter's not just materials but also transformative confidence boosting tools for his business, inspiring enthusiasm for their trustworthy performance capability. Not only did he pass that message on to his customers by showcasing the brand in his tile showroom, but he also boasted the exclusive use of the brand for all his installs in most of his advertising. Since Leo wins awards every year through the local building associations and certified remodelers' community, I can only imagine how that competitive analysis by his community also simulated growth for the Schluter brand as well. It's through trusted leaders and users brand messages are spread.

Consistency and education in brand growth

As years passed, Schluter's consistent branding and educational approach paid dividends. They became synonymous with waterproofing in the shower system industry, akin to how Kleenex is to tissues. Their decision to stick with their vibrant orange color and maintain uniformity in design reinforced their market presence. Their orange is so bright and visible during an installation, it is incredibly distinctive. Continually educating contractors, sponsoring events, and competitions, nationwide, Schluter ensured that their products became the trusted first choice, enhancing their reputation and reliability.

Sustainable brand strategy

Their strategy of avoiding retail distribution, using a dealer direct order system, followed by leveraging third-party distribution channels, displayed an understanding of operational efficiency and brand reach. Despite the availability of similar products, professionals in the field still refer to generic alternatives such as "Schluter," demonstrating the brand's dominant market position and the strength of its identity.

A blueprint for branding success

Schluter-Systems' journey from a German innovator to a staple in American construction highlights the power of a well-executed branding strategy. By aligning their visual identity with their UVP and maintaining consistency across all touchpoints, they have not only captured but also have continued to hold a commanding market share. Their story shows that subtle yet colorful branding, strategic marketing, and placement, as well as providing detailed installation education and support to users can lead to lasting success, influence, and referral sales generation where the product literally sells itself.

The vibrant exploration of color's profound influence on branding unlocked the secrets of visual identity that captivates and connects us on a psychological level with our audience. From the foundational strategies of selecting the right palette from my own experiences to the anecdotal success seen with brands like Schluter-Systems, it is just one example how a bold and integral color choice can sculpt a brand's image. In fact, over the years other companies have tried to recreate this same effective product color strategy by opting for bold colors to signify the brand without wording.

But the visual element is just part of the story. The final pillar, communication, displays how we can use the brand's framework (target persona and UVP) to enhance client engagement, leveraging the foundation laid by our visual and narrative branding efforts.

CHAPTER 4

Building Bonds Through Brand Architecture

Techniques for Engaging Clients and Selling with Attraction

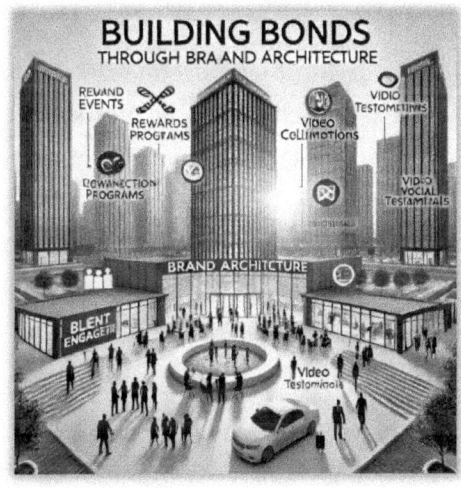

According to branding experts, after you have the foundational pillars and visual elements in place, the final critical pillar is communication.

As a solopreneur, the responsibility of crafting communication strategies remains with me, and it has lasted for several years. It's a familiar narrative among small businesses and entrepreneurs, who face the daunting statistic that many fail within the first three years. Attaining financial stability often takes just as much time. While savvy operators might enlist external resources for financial leverage, handing over our branding with a simple directive like, "Here you go, Mr. marketing subcontractor, please make sales for me" is ineffective and impractical.

A communication strategy requires as much diligence and approach as a football coach preparing for a big game. Just as a coach would only face a match prepared by analyzing past game tapes and/or scouting the opposition's strengths and weaknesses, we, too, must strategically plan our client engagement tactics.

And the standard sales strategies aren't effective anymore. The strategies developed by Rep Methods, on the other hand, shift my clients from reactive to proactive selling through a brand architecture. This approach isn't just about direct interaction; it leverages both human elements and technological tools, applying psychological branding principles to lighten the load of lead generation and sales pipeline maintenance while we continue to focus on our core work.

The strategy to create proactive sales begins with building a community around our brand. By reinforcing our UVP, our community can help us attract new clients and cultivate a network of referrals, reducing the reliance on traditional cold calls. Indeed, while cold calling, or as I prefer to call it "warm calling," remains a staple of business development, imagine a strategy that eases the burden off our entrepreneurial shoulders.

This comes through a variety of client engagement tactics. Engaging clients can be challenging. The engagement process is crucial, requiring a dynamic and iterative approach that involves constant analysis and refinement, which can be a daunting aspect of entrepreneurship.

Establishing a Brand Community

Creating a community is a proactive way to generate leads and referral business. It involves setting up online and in-person spaces for client interactions to accommodate their preferences. We can achieve community via social media, online networking platforms, opinion forums, and internal channels. Companies are making it increasingly difficult for consumers to engage in personalized interactions, which could negatively affect our society as we integrate robotic technology and AI.

I recently heard a story on NPR about a woman who runs a small community pharmacy in her city. She faces challenges competing with large pharmaceutical corporations and rising drug costs, where the "little guy" struggles to survive. She emphasized the importance of community engagement in her city. Given the limitations of her poverty-stricken community, personal support and open-door community engagement tactics are crucial for ensuring that clients receive proper assistance with medication instructions. With a strong community, her small mom-owned pharmacy could survive.

You can build community through social media and direct communication channels.

Social media community

In today's world, maintaining a social media presence is essential for businesses and brands, regardless of their size. According to BBC Online, video-based platforms such as TikTok and Instagram have significantly influenced consumers' purchasing decisions.[13] When researching a company or brand, most consumers typically start with the company's website or social media. The primary purpose of maintaining a social media presence for businesses is to influence sales and enable customers to influence others. Sara Karlovitch, an author at Marketingdrive.com, points out that 68 percent of consumers primarily use social media to stay informed about new products and services, highlighting the channel's potential for brands.[14]

"Social media is not just a virtual gathering place for friends and family—new research shows it's the epicenter of building brand-consumer trust, that requires timely, genuine engagement from brands."15 Finding and deciding which social media platforms to use is an ever-evolving challenge. According to Adobe, over two in five Americans use TikTok as a search engine, with nearly one in ten Zoomers relying more on TikTok than Google.16 Moreover, more than half of business owners use TikTok to promote their businesses, with one in four small business owners utilizing TikTok influencers for product sales or promotions.

Instead of employing a trial-and-error approach to creating your content, a more effective strategy is to analyze and learn

---

[13] Valeria Penttinen, "Why Are TikTok Creators So Good at Making People Buy Things," BBC Worklife, August 18, 2023,
https://www.bbc.com/worklife/article/20230818-why-are-tiktok-creators-so-good-at-making-people-buy-things.
[14] Sara Karlovitch, "Don't Miss Tomorrow's Marketing Industry News," Marketing Dive, accessed August 21, 2024,
https://www.marketingdive.com/editors/skarlovitch/.

[15] Sprout Social, "New Research Indicates a Shift in What Consumers Find Memorable on Social Media," last modified July 18, 2023,
https://investors.sproutsocial.com/news/news-details/2023/New-Research-Indicates-a-Shift-in-What-Consumers-Find-Memorable-on-Social-Media/default.aspx
[16] *Adobe Express*, accessed July 2024.
https://www.adobe.com/express/learn/blog/using-tiktok-as-a-search-engine.

from the competition. Identify similar companies or brands, evaluate their channels and content, and apply successful principles to your plan.

Along with that analysis, you need to keep your persona and a UVP in mind. Without these foundational pieces, we can be at the whims of social media's constantly changing trends and strategies. With them, we can use it to reach more customers, showcase our goals, influence purchasing decisions, and build a sense of trust in our brand.

Start by creating a group or a specific hashtag that aligns with your brand's UVP. Hashtags make our content accessible and easy to find across all platforms, channels, and outlets. They are a valuable resource for assessing performance and reaching new audiences.

Develop a comprehensive strategy using the three-pillar template: aspirational, call to action, and proof. Determine the percentage that best resonates with the target audience and adjust as needed. Unfortunately, these percentages are not exact due to the ever-changing algorithms on different platforms. Prepare to review and adjust quarterly based on shifts between pillars.

For example, if you are selling products online and expect a significant increase in sales during the holiday season, focus on creating a solid call-to-action approach months in advance and during the buying season. If your service-based brand has an off-season, adjust your content to focus more on the aspirational pillar during that time. For coaching businesses, it may be beneficial to emphasize the proof and aspirational pillars and let potential clients' calls to action come naturally.

Your posts should use attraction selling, a customer-centric approach, which prioritizes providing value and building meaningful relationships, helping to produce leads and create sales opportunities.

Create informative, educational content. You want your content to display products in a way that solves the client's problem.

Create personalized experiences. You do this by implementing a feeling of individuality, customization, and authenticity.

Authenticity forms the cornerstone of attraction selling and is one of the core responsibilities of social media for client engagement. By relying on the three-pillar methodology (**aspirational, call to action, proof**) instead of archaic sales pitches, you can focus on finding solutions for your customers while holding their attention long enough to present the call to action.

This section moves us forward to discussing strategies to turn customers into loyal fans who actively promote our business, helping to create a self-sustaining cycle of engagement and endorsement.

Video messaging. Ah, the age of the video, we are indeed in it! Generations are shopping on video channels, and the idea of photograph representation of how we do business is booming. With the rise of Instagram, TikTok, YouTube, and other platforms, utilizing personalized video messaging is not viable; it's survival. Entrepreneur.com wrote a funny and fantastic article in 2022 titled "You've Got 8 Seconds to Grab a Customer's Attention. Here's What to Do."[17] Inside, they discuss various

---

[17] Mike Kappel & Joseph Shults, "You've Got 8 Seconds to Grab a Customer's Attention. Here's What to Do," Entrepreneur.com, last modified June 26, 2022,

elements, from copy to bold designs to storytelling, simplicity, and ease of action. The attention span for Americans is down to three seconds from eight two years ago. Based on my analytics, the average person spends three to ten seconds on an online video. This helps us gauge if we've created engaging content. Interpreting data may seem daunting, but it's crucial for understanding customer engagement.

Keep in mind that it's more than just posting. It is about engaging and listening. When conducting competitive research and community listening, it's important to consider what the existing community is saying.

Community listening involves monitoring and analyzing online conversations about your product or brand, providing valuable insight and lead-generation opportunities. Responding promptly to the audience's comments, questions, feedback, and suggestions shows that you value their input and validate their opinions.

Using customer feedback and insights from performance, you can make informed decisions and demonstrate a customer-centric approach. You also foster a sense of belonging and loyalty, turning customers into active participants and brand ambassadors.

Social media isn't just a platform for outreach; it's a gold mine for gathering real-time customer insights. By actively listening to social media, businesses can tap into unfiltered conversations about their brand, industry, and competitors. This process involves monitoring mentions, hashtags, and discussions

---

https://www.entrepreneur.com/growing-a-busi ess/you've-got-8-sec nds-to-grab-a-customers-attention-heres/427827.

across various social platforms to understand public sentiment and gather feedback.

Implementing social media listening allows companies to identify trends, pinpoint customer pain points, and gauge overall satisfaction. It's also an excellent way to discover what customers appreciate most about your products or services and what aspects might need improvement. By analyzing this data, businesses can make informed decisions that align more closely with customer desires and market demands.

Moreover, social media provides a direct line to customer communication, enabling businesses to respond swiftly to inquiries, complaints, or praises. This responsiveness improves customer service and enhances brand loyalty and reputation. Engaging with customers demonstrates a company's commitment to listening to and adapting based on their feedback, fostering a stronger connection between the brand and its audience.

Incorporating social media listening into your strategy ensures that your business stays ahead of the curve by adapting to your target market's evolving needs and preferences. This will ultimately lead to enhanced customer relationships and increased business growth.

After collecting a wealth of data, the challenge—and indeed, the opportunity—lies in effectively interpreting and applying these insights to bring about meaningful change.

Craft personal responses. How about the "voice" of the brand and how you can personalize hitting your customers where it counts: their heart? Remember when you received a thank-you note whether handwritten or not. I recall a recent visit to the eye doctor, and weeks later, I received a small thank-you note in the mail thanking me for choosing their small business over a large chain. They let me know how valuable my visit was to their bottom line and made it clear that I had a choice and chose well.

Even if we don't want to go as far as relying on the USPS to mail our engagement, taking the time to craft a personal thank-you over email or even a phone call creates some loyalty magic, I can't explain.

According to Harvard Health, an online blog from Harvard Medical School, "Writing thank-you notes is not simply manners. It can have a strong psychological effect for both the sender and receiver."[18]

Facilitate direct communication channels

Starting a Facebook group for my "sales club" required little or no effort, and I hastily began recruiting a few hundred participants! Offering discounts, special programs, and special events from this free resource is one effortless way to use social media to build a community.

My website host program also has an impressive group function for customers. By using the preset protocols, when customers subscribe to my online presence, I can offer automated responses to encourage participation. This interactive area where clients engage with each other on my website is a slightly more controlled environment than social media but

---

[18] "Writing a Thank-You Note Is More Powerful Than You Think," Harvard Health Publishing, last modified November 20, 2018,
https://www.health.harvard.edu/mind-and-mood/writing-a-thank-you-note-is-more-powerful-than-you-think.

provides the same direct communication and community listening opportunities.

Consider affixing a live chat function on your website or even a feedback form on the Contact Us page, making it easy for clients to send comments or requests.

Create these segments across multiple channels to capture the bulk of your audience. Take a diverse approach and refer to the target persona and UVP to find coherent channels.

One of my favorite techniques for facilitating direct communication is polls! It's incredible to see how many people are ready to give their opinion about something. When we make it easy by simplifying the opinion down to "choose a, b, or c," the response probability goes way up. According to Elaine Walsh-McGrath via LinkedIn, "Polls and Surveys serve as interactive gateways to your audience's thoughts, preferences, and pain points. They spark engagement and provide invaluable insights that can shape your content strategy and offerings."[19]

Other avenues for community building

Get involved in existing channels! The plethora of groups and forums might eliminate the need to create one. According to an online source, "Platforms like Reddit, Quora, or specialized forums related to your industry can provide a platform to connect with individuals who are enthusiastic about specific topics."[20]

---

[19] Elaine Walsh-McGrath, "Maximizing Engagement: The Art of Polls and Surveys," LinkedIn, accessed July 26, 2024,
https://www.linkedin.com/pulse/maximizing-engagement-art-polls-surveys-linkedin-elaine-walsh-mcgrath-cypge/.
[20] "Reaching Your Target Audience," Fastercapital.com, accessed July 2024. https://fastercapital.com/topics/reaching-our-target-audience.html/2

I've enjoyed finding industry groups, buying groups, "working the room," and listening to and engaging with my community managed by other parties. I also try to collaborate with leaders in creating video content whenever possible. Once that communication strategy is formulated, we can use our strengths to broadcast digitally. Here's a quick story of one collaboration effort in progress with one of the tech companies I am using in my marketing, *Deep Reel*[21]

Case Study – Collaboration Deep Reel & Rep Methods

The CEO of Deep Reel got in touch with me after I sent feedback communication during a creative day in the office making videos about this new book. I decided to incorporate avatars in my communication strategy. Long story short, while communicating with the company one on one, we decided to establish a community opportunity by formulating an interview we could both use on our YouTube channels and or Deep Reel's frequently asked questions area on the web. Using AI, I was able to create a script and facility questions communicating both our sales interests: Deep Reel wants to find and showcase more small business entrepreneurs like me, and I want to show my audience how conducting this type of interview is a way to sell, without selling. For fun, let me insert show you the final script and maybe you can use this idea in finding a similar collaboration and build community on both sides of the coin.

---

[21] Beta.deepreel.com

Specialty Segment: Deep Reel & Rep Methods: "Beyond Order Makers" Entrepreneur Technology Segment—The Use of Avatars in Marketing

Introduction

- **Host (Deep Reel Representative):** "Welcome to a special edition of our Deep Reel Entrepreneur Technology Segment. Today, we're honored to have Alison Mullins, the owner of Rep Methods LLC and bestselling author of *The Art of Selling: We Make Order Makers, Not Order Takers*. In this segment, we'll explore the transformative power of avatar technology in modern marketing and how solo entrepreneurs can use it to grow their brands. Alison, thanks for joining us today!"
- **Alison:** [Briefly introduces herself and mentions the release of her new book, *Beyond Order Makers*, which focuses on innovative marketing strategies.]

Section 1: Addressing a Key Challenge - Entrepreneurs and Camera Shyness

- **Host:** "Alison, in your experience, many entrepreneurs face the challenge of being on camera. Whether it's discomfort or simply a preference to stay behind the scenes, it's a common barrier. How do you see Deep Reel Avatars addressing this challenge?"

- **Alison:** [Speaks about the hesitation many feel when being on camera and how Deep Reel Avatars offer an ideal solution, allowing entrepreneurs to communicate confidently without stepping in front of the lens.]
- **Host:** "And in your book *The Art of Selling*, you emphasize the importance of clear and authentic messaging. Can avatars really help maintain that sense of authenticity with the audience?"
- **Alison:** [Discusses how avatars can still create authentic connections when the messaging is clear and consistent, emphasizing that the value lies in delivering the right message effectively.]

Section 2: Deep Reel's Integration with Canva - A Game-Changer for Content Creation

- **Host:** "Let's talk about Deep Reel's integration with Canva. Canva has become the go-to tool for entrepreneurs creating visual content. How does this combination streamline content creation for solo entrepreneurs?"
- **Alison:** [Explains the synergy between Canva and Deep Reel, highlighting the ability to pair professional visuals with avatar-driven narration, making it easier for entrepreneurs to create cohesive marketing videos without specialized skills.]
- **Host:** "For solo entrepreneurs, saving time and maximizing creativity is crucial. Could you share a few use cases where an entrepreneur might use this integration to market a new product or, say, promote a bestselling book like *Beyond Order Makers*?"
- **Alison:** [Provides specific examples, such as promotional videos for product launches, short video ads,

book trailers, and brand storytelling content using custom visuals paired with avatar presentations.]

Section 3: High-Quality Marketing on a Minimalist Budget

- ▸ **Host:** "Budget constraints are a common concern for small businesses. How does Deep Reel help entrepreneurs create high-quality marketing videos without the high costs usually associated with videography and production?"
- ▸ **Alison:** [Highlights the affordability of Deep Reel Avatars, how they offer professional-quality content at a fraction of the cost, and how they eliminate the need for renting equipment or hiring external talent.]
- ▸ **Host:** "In your book, *Beyond Order Makers*, you talk about the shift from flashy budgets to smart, effective communication. How does Deep Reel align with this new mindset in marketing?"
- ▸ **Alison:** [Discusses how Deep Reel Avatars allow entrepreneurs to focus on storytelling and delivering impactful messages, rather than investing heavily in production costs.]

Section 4: The Professionalism and Authenticity of Avatar-Driven Videos

- ▸ **Host:** "Professionalism and authenticity are key in building trust with an audience. How can entrepreneurs ensure that their Deep Reel Avatars reflect these values in their videos?"

- **Alison:** [Discusses the customizable features of avatars, including tone, style, and script alignment, to create an experience that resonates authentically with viewers.]
- **Host:** "What would you say to entrepreneurs who may be hesitant about using avatars, wondering if they might come off as less genuine or robotic?"
- **Alison:** [Reassures hesitant entrepreneurs by emphasizing advancements in AI, improvements in avatar expressions, and the strategic importance of focusing on consistent messaging to build authenticity.]

Section 5: How Entrepreneurs Can Leverage Avatars to Close More Sales

- **Host:** "Your bestselling book, *The Art of Selling*, focuses on creating 'Order Makers' instead of just 'Order Takers'. How can leveraging avatar-driven videos help entrepreneurs close more deals and convert prospects into loyal customers?"
- **Alison:** [Shares insights about the importance of guiding the audience towards a decision, the psychology of clear calls-to-action, and how avatars can effectively present these cues in a consistent, engaging way.]
- **Host:** "Could you share a practical tip or example from your new book, *Beyond Order Makers*, on using avatar videos to create a strong call to action?"
- **Alison:** [Offers a specific strategy or example, such as scripting a concise call-to-action that uses urgency or value-based language to inspire immediate viewer engagement.]

Chapter 4

Section 6: Ideas for the Future - Evolving Avatar Technology

- **Host:** "Alison, you're known for your forward-thinking approach to business. Where do you see avatar technology, like Deep Reel's, evolving in the future? What innovations would you love to see next?"
- **Alison:** "One idea I'm particularly excited about is using Deep Reel Avatars to collect customer testimonials. Imagine allowing customers to provide written or verbal feedback, and having avatars present those stories in a way that's consistent with your brand. This would be a powerful way to showcase social proof and build trust without requiring customers to be on camera. It's about creating more opportunities to capture and share authentic experiences."
- **Host:** "That's an exciting idea! It would make collecting and presenting social proof so much easier for entrepreneurs. We're thrilled to see where Deep Reel can go with this in the future."

Section 7: Final Thoughts and Future Trends

- **Host:** "As we wrap up, where do you see the future of avatar technology going, and how can entrepreneurs stay ahead of the curve in using these tools effectively?"
- **Alison:** [Discusses the broader trends in AI, personalization in digital marketing, and the importance of staying adaptable and open to new technologies in maintaining a competitive edge.]
- **Host:** "Thank you so much for sharing your insights, Alison. For those of you watching, if you're looking for a professional and innovative way to present your brand

without being on camera, Deep Reel Avatars are worth exploring. And be sure to check out Alison's book, *Beyond Order Makers*, for more actionable strategies on turning your marketing into sales."

Closing Call-to-Action

> **Host:** "To learn more about Deep Reel Avatars or start using them in your videos today, visit our website at DeepReel.com. And don't forget to subscribe to our channel for more tips on elevating your marketing game. Thanks for watching!"

How do you feel about this type of approach? Could you see yourself finding a brand collaborator?

I loved creating an opportunity for both Deep Reel and Rep Methods to benefit from the casual sales pitch without selling! We highlighted both of our target personas, communicated our point of view and subtly showcased the UVP of both brands, in a conversation.

I'm thrilled I get to help make technology better, too! Working with Sahil, communicating my needs as a small business owner is a great way to help his business grow. I hope one day someone will help us business owners find easier ways to collect testimonials. Gathering feedback and establishing ways to collect testimonials is a common sales theme you will find as you continue reading this chapter and subsequent chapters.

Chapter 4

Establish Monitoring Tools & Data Collection

Reviews and feedback. I enlist the help of programs like Trustpilot to encourage starred reviews and commentary, which I can use when creating aspirational graphics for my social channels. You can position these reviews and testimonials on your brand visuals to help encourage and support positivity around your brand. Another obvious option? Feedback forms are a guaranteed way of hearing from your customers. While getting your clients to fill them out is difficult, businesses often use coupons, or specialty offers to entice interactions.

Connecting customer feedback analysis directly to implementation underscores a proactive business strategy, emphasizing customer satisfaction and ongoing development. This approach resolves immediate concerns and builds a culture of responsiveness and adaptability, which is crucial for entrepreneurs and salespeople aiming to deepen customer relationships and enhance their competitive edge.

The first step is organizing the feedback into relevant categories. Organizing feedback helps align responses and can reveal patterns that suggest how we might improve our processes or policies. For example, sorting the data helped me realize that my seminar content was overly extensive, prompting a necessary focus and trimming of topics.

Next, prioritize and thoroughly examine the impact of each piece of feedback. Ask yourself: Which elements have the most significant impact on customer satisfaction and business performance? Can these impacts be quantified? To determine the optimal number of topics for a half-day seminar, quantify the time allotted for each subject. This analysis assists you in deciding which topics are essential and which can be omitted to improve the program's effectiveness.

It's also invaluable to cross-reference feedback with actual performance metrics or presentation outcomes. This approach lets you pinpoint which topics resonate most and which fail to engage your audience. In my case, recalling and removing less relevant issues streamlined the content and improved the overall quality and focus of my seminars.

If you have a team, engage them in the process! We all know how staff love to give their opinions on how things must be done. It's important to consider that information and collect insights from all parties involved. You can then use this information to turn your customers into brand advocates.

Turning customers into brand advocates relies on customer appreciation and using the messages from our clients to highlight that we are a trusted entity. Video plays a role here too— it's not just gathering the words anymore. How often have you been reading Amazon product reviews and thinking—"that's fake." I can't stress authenticity enough; I don't buy into purchased reviews or soliciting fake feedback. It doesn't work. A decade ago, posting a written testimonial on a website was sufficient. However, in today's market, how long will websites be relevant?

Video testimonials are all the rage; new technology platforms make gathering them more accessible daily. These communication elements are the current trend in resonating deeply with customers. We can also control how these fantastic little attraction-selling nuggets are released. Consider holding on to them or sending them in customer-specific lead emails. Sometimes I use them in funnels designed to get the prospect over the hurdle of consideration. If a prospect is partially on the hook but won't commit, these fantastic quick videos can often push the decision in your favor. And if we're lucky, AI and technology will continue to help us make this information collection technique easier to gather.

Analytics and SEO. Google offers free analytics if you have a registered business with them. I employ a program called Semrush[22] to help evaluate the SEO and performance keywords within the website. While I never wanted to claim to be an SEO expert, I have learned a lot about the subject. To quickly summarize, it's how our websites vie for a search ranking. It determines what number or page our website shows up on when customers go to a search engine and perform a search to find a business to interact with for purchases or service bookings.

Based on the internet algorithms, adding keywords in specific quantities throughout a website can influence how high we rank. The importance and relevance of SEO for your business are entirely related to how easily you aspire to be found in the world of Google and beyond. I will mention this later and quote it here: the internet is no longer the optimum search engine for business, and social media is the current leader. I cannot predict how long this will be relevant. Nevertheless, I find it necessary to stress to my audience the importance of incorporating SEO and data analytics into our monthly and quarterly monitoring.

---

[22] https://www.semrush.com/

Host Special Events Online or Offline—Maximize ROI

Creating special customer-only events is one of my favorite methods for enlisting customer engagement. We can weave in some data collection into our event planning, deepening our understanding of our clients and industry peers and highlighting a commitment to continual improvement.

Leveraging personalized events and data collection enhances the value of these gatherings and significantly boosts the return on investment for your business development efforts. This approach ensures that every interaction counts toward building a more responsive and attuned business.

In my experience, people love to show up for free stuff! Food, beverages, door prizes, raffles, auctions, and celebrity meetings are a few enticing attractions we can use to get our customers to engage with us in person.

Hosting events and workshops. Doing this presents a unique opportunity to deepen lead engagement and personalize customer interactions, as they provide a platform for brands to highlight products or services and engage with customers more personally, even online! However, to ensure the success of these events and achieve a positive return on investment, you need to first listen to the community and cater to their needs.

One effective way to gather insights and tailor in-store events is by actively listening to customer feedback through various channels, including surveys, focus groups, and social media monitoring. We can gain insights into what customers want and need by soliciting input before, during, and after events, allowing them to tailor their offerings accordingly.

For example, suppose a retail store specializing in skincare products hosts a workshop on skincare routines. In that case, they can customize the event's content and format with customer feedback. Customers may express interest in learning about specific skincare ingredients or techniques, which the store can incorporate into the workshop agenda. By addressing these specific needs and interests, the store not only enhances the value of the event for attendees but also increases the likelihood of generating leads and driving sales.

Another example is hosting a workshop on sales techniques (ahem!) and inviting your customer base to partake in the special event. Remember that everyone is selling something. **What extra exceptional value can you offer customers? Can you offer them a chance to learn something to help them grow?** Arranging a work-based workshop that benefits both the host and the attendees maximizes lead engagement—buying and creating valued time to spend with your customers and learning about their needs. Within the kitchen and bath industry, this is a regular practice. Wholesalers and retailers host continuing education events for the design community to give these customers a reason to want to enter their space. By creating and buying these specifiers time, they created opportunities for them to see and return to them for a purchase.

However, you can't just create the event and pray it all works out. How can you make these opportunities even more impactful? Can you guarantee results?

I once participated in event coordination for a holiday event where the wholesaler spent a couple of months planning and refining budgets, decorations, food, and theme, and the result was a fun, festive, beautifully planned event for the clients. In the end, two designers showed up for the event. Two. It was a disaster. The week before the event, I asked the coordinator if I could help with the RSVP list and head count. I wasn't in charge, but I began to panic for the store when we discovered they only had fifteen RSVPs. In my experience, only 30 percent of RSVPs attend an event. So, if you'd like to have fifty attendees for a party, you need to invite two hundred people and have 166 RSVPs. Less experienced showroom staffers make the most common errors. So, how do you avoid this pitfall of hosting in-person events?

You make an RSVP execution plan. Before the decor or catering begins to plan, you must prepare your attendee lists and plan how to secure, follow up, and enforce the *yes* to the RSVP! What's an RSVP execution plan you might ask? Well, if applicable, using your outside sales team and utilizing their time to physically deliver an invitation or a phone call invitation is a successful start. First, start with that detailed list of invitees. Perhaps put a few into categories such as high priority, special guests, honored guests, general attendees, and supporting organizations. Next, create physical and virtual invitations with clearly defined RSVP instructions. While we can do our best to outline how we want guests to RSVP, the real work is following up post-invite to make sure that happens. I suggest setting a few deadlines and a timeline for both RSVP success and accurate follow-up. Then, outline when and how you will follow up accordingly. I strongly recommend using the phone to follow up. Try giving the client the option of having you fill out the online RSVP for them! Doesn't it always feel like people are asking you to click this, fill out that? Try doing the work for them and see if that increases the overall response ratio.

Chapter 4

> **Pro tip:** Use the phone to gather RSVP's—filling out any online RSVP links for the client, making it easy for them to say YES!

One other point, and perhaps most important of all: before hosting an event to buy your customers' time and create a solitary engagement scenario, check other events happening the same day/night. Selecting the right date and timing for an event is setting yourself up for success from the planning stage. A quick story.

Event planning fail

Once upon a time, in a sales position long long ago, I worked for a company who wanted to host an amazing holiday bash drawing in our luxury designer target customer as well as embracing our everyday winning customers who were quite familiar with visiting our facility on a regular basis. We really wanted to pull in the specification crowd, a group not easily drawn in to visit regularly. I still remember the devastation and failed ROI because our event planner failed to check the local networking groups, industry association and general event schedule for the area. On the same night we wanted to draw in the luxury designer audience, we found out there was another special event the same night! Not just any event, but a black-tie awards gala for this specific architecture & designer community! How could we expect this crowd to choose our event over the fancy gala at a fancy hotel with fancy tickets purchased in advance? We were destined for failure before we began. Lesson learned. Take note to check the regional events before selecting a date.

*Special Note—you will deduce clearer ideas on where to cross-check within your community once you have completed the target marketing work in section two. I can't wait to help you begin to win before you've even hired a caterer!

Online events. These should include educational sessions, informal happy hours, or, for example, one of my industry communities provides a power hour filled with variable industry insights. [23] Online events are a great way to capture the attention of our target audience without asking them to "go" anywhere! Don't forget to make it easy for them to say yes by ensuring you have an ask that fulfils their specific needs and to help them say yes by following up and offering to have food and beverages delivered as if they were at a catered event.

Now that I've given you some amazing ways to build bonds within your community, let's review and take note of my personal event checklist.

Event planning checklist

- What's the main event going to be?
- Is there an eye-catching person, award, raffle, speaker, gift to draw people in?
- What else is going on around town?
- Who do you want to attend? (Don't say everyone)
- How many people do you ideally want to entertain? Divide by 30 percent to reveal the number of RSVPs required.
- Develop a plan for invitation personalization delivery.

---

[23] "Online Events," Women In The Floorcovering Industry (WIFI), accessed June 21, 2024, https://www.womeninflooring.org/power-hour.

- Develop and have enough time for adequate follow-up.
    - Six weeks out
    - Four weeks out
    - Two weeks out
    - Week of event
- Plan for collecting customer data during the event and having a survey ready to post to gather feedback.

Overall, online and in-store events allow businesses to engage in meaningful customer conversations, further deepening relationships and fostering trust. By actively listening to customers during these interactions, business owners can uncover valuable insights about their customers' preferences, pain points, and purchasing behaviors. This information can tailor future interactions and personalize marketing efforts, increasing customer satisfaction and loyalty. Hopefully, with this checklist in tow, you can find better ways to build in that automatic ROI and make the in-person events a regularly themed method of client engagement and deepening lead engagement.

Create Reward Systems

In my work as a sales trainer and coach, the reward system typically involves customer discounts for repeat clients and or returning customers. Often, when renewing a contract, I'll apply a 10– 20 percent discount off the list price to help encourage the feeling of belonging and mutual respect for the ongoing relationship. Engaging customers in the status of business while initiating a reward helps keep them returning for more.

Last but not least, if you are unsure if you've finalized all the brand architecture necessities, try using this checklist to fill in any gaps.

Client Engagement Checklist with Brand Architecture

- ☐ Have you clearly defined a target persona?
- ☐ Have you crafted UVP statement(s)?
- ☐ Is the UVP communicated across all platforms?
- ☐ Does your brand have a story?
- ☐ Are your logo, colors, and design elements consistent across all platforms?
- ☐ Do all visual elements align with the target persona and UVP?
- ☐ Have you established a brand voice? Guidelines?
- ☐ Have you chosen two or three companies as competitive landscapes for comparison?
- ☐ What communication channels work best with the target persona? (ex: Email, social media, in-person events, radio advertising, direct mail)
- ☐ Have you defined your audience's preferred social networks?
- ☐ Have you identified all the touchpoints where customers interact with your brand?
- ☐ Do you have systems in place to gather customer feedback?
- ☐ Do you have measures in place to collect analytics?
- ☐ Do you have a schedule to review the data and feedback collected regularly?
- ☐ How often do you believe you will need to refresh this strategy?
- ☐ What are the "community" options relevant to your brand?
- ☐ Is there a strategy in place to implement this strategy?

Chapter 4

Final Note: Brand Resilience, Navigating Challenges with Grace

Luckily, my forte has always been business development. It's as if I was born with a knack for navigating the intricate world of networking and cooperative branding and consistently casting a wide yet refined net—constantly working to retain and slowly expand the client base. That doesn't mean that brand development and maintaining resilience don't come with challenges.

You need a solid foundation when storms hit. As entrepreneurs, resilience goes beyond surviving tough times; it's about excelling amid challenges. And it starts with understanding and effectively communicating your UVP. As a salesperson, aligning my pitch with the brand's resilient UVP becomes paramount during turbulence—whether because of economic shifts, evolving consumer preferences, or PR. Showing adaptability and emphasizing the brand's value proposition helps weather challenges and thrive.

As a sales training coach, I often wonder whether all this foundational "brand" work is already in place when taking on a new client. It's separate from the teaching regimen because we already have so much work to do regarding the sales process and becoming a proactive seller. If you've diligently done your homework and clarified the long-term vision, you should feel as though you've just awakened on the deck of a boat in the Pacific Islands—where the sky is clear, the air is crisp, and you can see miles ahead beyond the storms you've weathered. Finally, you will be there soon.

While it's a godsend when salespeople already inherit solid branding, a distinct voice, and an engaged community, we often need help navigating business development's complexities! Many small businesses struggle to craft the proper outreach and spend too much time in the wrong markets.

You can improve your business development by refining sales techniques, learning how to prioritize and personalize your approach to clients, and perfecting relationships.

I urge you to use what you learned in this chapter to discover ways to transform customers and casual browsers into valuable referrals. Leveraging the voices of clients who become as passionate about our business as we are, is crucial. As a solopreneur, these advocates are not just valuable for someone like me—they're essential to my business's survival. By implementing the strategies discussed, you can turn casual customers into staunch advocates, ensuring every satisfied client becomes a beacon for your brand and extends its reach and impact beyond typical marketing efforts. Embrace these techniques to survive and thrive by turning passion into advocacy.

SECTION 2

Mastering Target Marketing

Unlocking Business Development

CHAPTER 5

Beyond the Octopus

Target Marketing and Prioritization

Do you remember trying to write a paper for English class, maybe in high school? Do you remember how annoying it was when our English teachers forced us to outline before diving into the actual writing? If like me, you found stopping to backup and outlining my work annoying, then this chapter is for you! Buckle your seat belts and get out those post it's, this chapter is packed with various outlining and visualization strategies, which you might find just that, *annoying*. But please be merciful as we get through this. It works and it has helped hundreds thus far. At the end of this chapter I've got a big case study for you to apply all that you will learn in this chapter, but before we begin, a little history:

Chapter 5

Mind mapping

This powerful visualizer emerges as a powerful tool in business, not just for entrepreneurs focused on sales and revenue generation, but for salespeople who struggle with large territories and never seem to have enough time or organization. In this chapter we will apply this technique by visually organizing our ideas to tackle the challenges of sales, targeting customers and with confidence, scale our business.

If you read my previous book, *The Art of Selling, We Make Order Makers, Not Order Takers,* you may remember the innovative "octopus diagram" I created for mind mapping target marketing. This tool has not only caught on, but has become indispensable. My clients now use hundreds of these diagrams. They're tucked into productivity binders, pinned on cork boards, and sketched on scraps of paper across offices worldwide. This simple, yet effective, tool has proven invaluable in helping salespeople and entrepreneurs visualize and secure new business relationships, drawing clients into their focus, hence the tentacle reference.

It's time to stop the cycle of spinning your wheels wondering who, where, and how you are going to find clients and *make orders.*

In section one, we've laid out a great map for branding and a marketing strategy and ultimately scrutinized a target persona of **who and why we designed this business in the first place.** But does that translate to an action strategy for sales? Not yet. The practice of mind mapping will help us narrow down our sales strategy and our business development targets. You can stop ending up in the proverbial weeds. Like a culinary team struggling to keep pace during the seven o'clock rush hour, poor target marketing mirrors this chaos: lack of time, unsure where to start our day or what to do next. Let's end the mystery and squirreled chaos. Choose to overperform and underpromise yourself by trying to reach every inch of the market and, instead, start slowly with extreme target marketing and limit your reach! Expansion will come with time.

Often, I interact with sales managers and owners, focusing solely on increasing revenue. *Get the highest revenue possible*!

Yes, we should focus on increasing revenue; however, we should also:

- design a sales strategy that narrows our focus
- stop stretching ourselves thin for the wrong type of client or business
- get out of our comfort zone but with a more selective approach
- abandon the pursuit of time-sucking wastes of effort that don't produce the proper revenue and frankly keep us "spinning our wheels" in the wrong direction

Ideally, we need to find clients we *want* to work with who ultimately keep us snowballing in the right direction, building on connections and networks.

To do that, we're going to start by creating a **master octopus diagram** and following advanced techniques for **prioritization**, providing insights into effective **resource allocation** and **time-management strategies**. By utilizing these deeper-dive methods, businesses can elevate their **marketing efforts both in person and digitally, strengthen networking strategies**, and, most importantly, **protect precious resources like time, money, and energy.**

Have you ever heard of a "squirrel" mentality? When it comes to my industry, this is a common adjective I use and have heard other people use when our people lose focus and concentration often. The result is commonly reactive selling practices such as spending time answering emails more often than generating offers. Or when we are chasing poor leads rather than curating solid leads. Often, salespeople who don't address their squirrel mentality can get stuck forever chasing "anything that moves".

What is a "squirrel" mentality?

Have you ever seen the movie *Up*, a Pixar film?

Dug, the dog, struggles to focus during conversations with his beloved owner. Dug's owner gifted him a collar that could "speak" his thoughts, but every thought was constantly interrupted by the *"squirrel"*. Without proper focus and targeted planning, entrepreneurs and salespeople can easily lose direction and become distracted. It's the difference between being a reactive salesperson and a proactive salesperson. **Don't be an order taker; be an order maker**.

My approach deviates from atypical reactive selling tactics commonly seen in traditional business development roles, which are mostly uncovered in underperforming sales associates. I support proactive sales techniques. Start with the data you already own, seek to prioritize, magnify those solid customers and begin to expand slowly.

The first step in this process is to create a master diagram representing all categories of customers you might do business with. Don't worry, we'll get into prioritization and customized reach later.

Begin by looking at your sales history data. Think about any 'groups' you could place these customers, maybe there are some industry groups or other demographic category to group them together. Then, start thinking about all the adjacent industries or groups that touch the primary ones? For example, in my line of work, training salespeople, I want to work with sales representatives within the construction materials industry. I know I have the most influence and direct relationship to help transform teams that also sell construction materials. Now, based on knowing who my main demographic is, I start by identifying those core customer groups and then try to open my mind and find some parallel opportunities. So, I'll begin by showing you an example blank target market diagram. Don't worry, you'll have a chance to do one on your own soon.

Chapter 5

Master Target Market

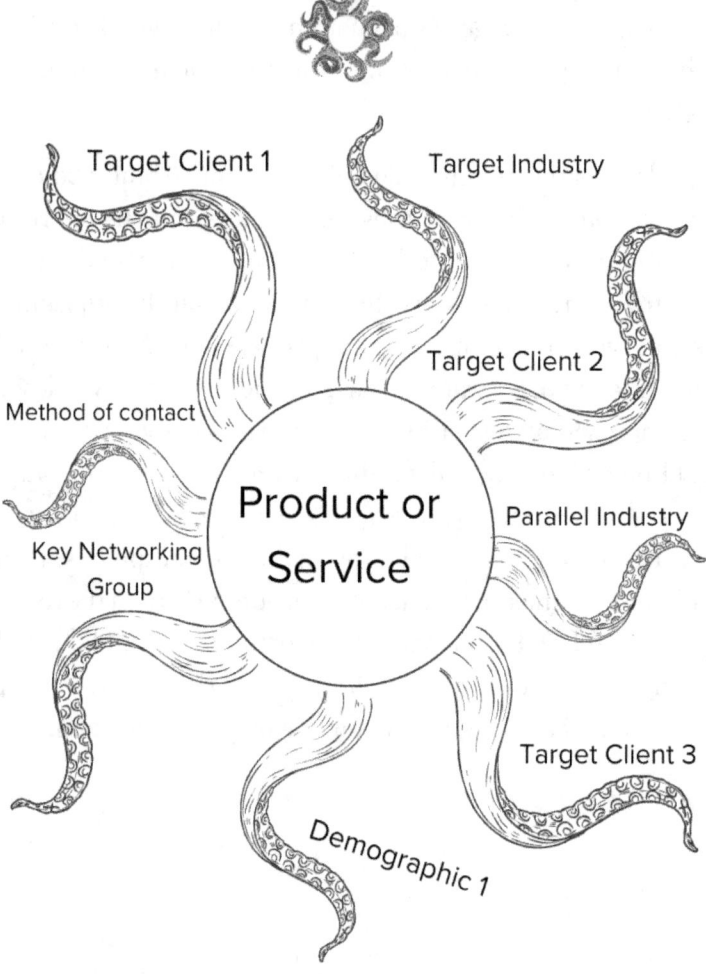

As you can see there are eight arms of customer categories, feel free to double up on your own if necessary, as eight arms might not be enough. You may notice a couple of things right away, and you might even begin to get a little excited during this discovery process.

> **Pro tip!** Use ChatGPT as a research assistant once you have completed a diagram or two. ChatGPT can help find parallel demographics or industries you can't see.

Try one on your own, using a pencil, not a pen. I'm inserting a blank version for you to begin on your own. If you decide you want more blank copies, simply draw them, or write to me and I'll send you the files.

Completing your first master diagram, you might find there are far more potential client categories than you realized! This is good news! You'll have a chance to work on them one by one if you so choose. But don't get to excited too quickly as later in this section I'll show you how to prioritize and block out those "spinning wheels" obstacles.

Congratulations! You are on your way to seeing out of the darkness and opening more opportunities for you to start selling right away. Hang these up in your office, and whenever you don't seem to know where to find that next sale, simply look up at the wall.

Chapter 5

Target Clients

Moving on, it's time to prioritize. We've started to create a space to find a lot of new customers we never knew existed or perhaps were lost in the time and space continuum. With our octopus diagrams we have a more complete vision of not only who, but in some cases how we can increase our network right away. I want to give you a great shot at buying back some of that wasted time and effort, so let's start to prioritize these customers and groups and give clients a rank as we find them, so we know right where they fit into our plan of attack.

Beyond Order Making: Prioritization for Business Development and Focus

The idea here is to apply real-life sales data and knowledge you already have into real-life data you can use to formulate a better sales strategy. Maybe there is a client category you haven't seen before. For example, the mobile notary business. Thanks to the help of my friend Bill Soroka during my first book launch, I learned of a new category of sales trainees coming from an industry I have never worked with before.

For me, one great parallel industry I discovered is "shed industry" retailers. Last year I met Shannon Latham, through a podcast call. Shannon runs the Shed Geek Podcast. Shannon brought me an entirely new client category! I could never have found this industry without Shannon's help and got me thinking in terms of a whole new diagram! As a networking king and communication leader serving his community, Shannon helped me discover the need for sales training spreads wider than the entrepreneur and small businesses I created my initial business plan.

Chapter 5

You see, when we mix parallel demographics or industries into our brand strategy work, we often find our products and services can reach beyond that target persona. But before we go off to the races to make more diagrams, keep on prioritizing and slow down for a minute to rank these customers based on quality of revenue and efficiency.

Create a detailed customer priority list

Our next step in the target marketing organization process is to start pulling together a report of current clients and existing business accounts you visit regularly, then start adding in any old accounts or lost business from the past. Try to make the most comprehensive client list possible. If you don't have a CRM that can quickly pull this data for you, start with a simple list in Excel. Another way to get a list started is by exporting client data from your website. Or you can try pulling clients from accounting software or even an email system; either way, this initial list exists somewhere! In the worst-case scenario, create a simple Excel spreadsheet if you are brand new. If you'd like, you can start with something like the charts below, where the last column asks you to rank your current customers based on revenue quality and efficiency.

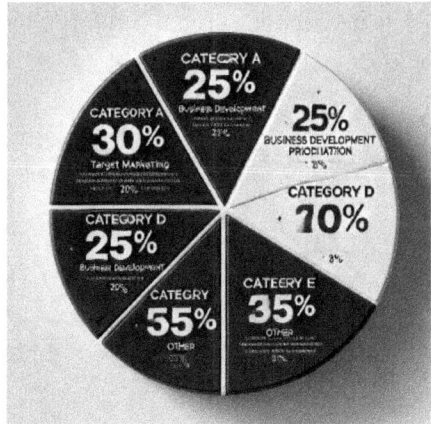

Next, go down the list ranking each client as A, B, C, D, and E. Rankings should be considered based on these revenue and time efficiency questions:

- Who brings you the fastest and most efficient type of revenue?
- Who (specific or category) do you aspire to work with and build more business because of the aspiration of a big payoff?
- Who is your next best "ease of doing business" customer?
- Who are the clients you don't want to turn away from but must be careful not to overspend your time?
- Who are the clients you can do without?

Assigning categories to the current prospect list and making sure to add aspirational account categories help us begin to define a real-time business development plan. For fun, let's use some jargon terms to start naming and discussing our target market groups. These are meant to be ideas only! If you wish, make up your own names to describe the revenue stream from each category.

Chapter 5

Low-Hanging Fruit—Fastest, most uncomplicated revenue, not necessarily high value.

Cash Cows—Clients who can bring in substantial revenue with minimal effort.

Rock Solid Blue Chips—Highly reliable, valuable clients with strong financial stability and consistent projects.

Repeat Offenders—Clients frequently return for more services or products, sometimes providing difficult or slow opportunities but reliable business associates.

Value Seekers/Skeptics—One-time, one-off clients who are unlikely to return or become a brand advocate. These clients require convincing and reassurance before making a purchase.

If you are having trouble identifying categories, try using the pareto principle—"80 percent of outcomes come from 20 percent of causes."[24] Thus, 80 percent of your business will come from 20 percent of your clients, so 80 percent of your time and money should be spent on 20 percent of your business targets while you let the rest come to fruition naturally.

---

[24] Richard Koch, *The 80/20 Principle: The Secret to Achieving More with Less* (New York: Currency, 1998), 4-7.

(B2C) Target Marketing & Prioritization Table

Client First Name	Client Last Name	DEMOGRAPHIC one	DEMOGRAPHIC two	Ranking (A, B, C, D, E, F)

(B2B) Target Marketing & Prioritization Table

Client Business Name	Client Primary Industry	Any Subcategory Or Demographic	Parallel Industry	Ranking (A, B, C, D, E, F)

Case Study: ICAA for Grassi Pietre

Grassi Pietre is the limestone company I contract my business development skills part time to stay connected to the industry and help one of my sisters in the stone industry Mariavittoria Grassi. I use my own principles all the time in this work, and a great example of how prioritization helps me in this practice is using an industry organization to help me find qualified leads for our business. I apply this practice to the membership data from within a very specific organization called the Institute for Classical Architecture and Art, ie. ICAA. This group meets all our qualifications and exemplifies the exact target market we hope to reach nationwide. When it comes time for me to focus on outreach in a territory, I cross reference and categorize the members based on fit to our profile. I rank them according to if we are likely to get specified or be selected for consideration and allows me to target my outreach and eliminates a lot of wasted time in messaging that goes nowhere. If you aren't in our industry, I will explain a bit further and clarify I could easily mass email and try to reach every architect in the state of Florida, but what would that do? Bother people unnecessarily, create spam emails that clog inboxes, and inevitably waste people's time who are not inclined to use this companies' product. By taking my time, slowing down and recognizing our true target market, I'm able to work faster, more efficiently and able to time block my outreach so it doesn't interfere with my day to day running two businesses.

With that realistic example, hopefully you can see the advantages of taking this extra step and hopefully you've already started a nifty master client list.

Now, it's time to go back to the octopus and see if you've missed any demographic or industry that maybe you didn't think of at first. It also helps to start talking to industry leaders by networking in small business groups or online communities. Just double check and don't forget to ask for help from AI or a third party. We can't always see what we can't see.

Create a master reach diagram.

This is where you get to envision how you to create sales interactions and build out your attraction selling plan. We spent quite a bit of time in section one preparing you for how to mix in the data we would discover during section two, right? Making orders and generating sales reach isn't simply marketing with social media and advertising, it requires us to communicate both digitally and in person or over the phone.

What—you didn't imagine yourself interacting with your client? Well, my friend, sales might be tough for you.

And hey, business owner, not ready to get out and start networking, well, my friend, sales will be tough for you.

In other words, without *organic reach*, without *consistent touches* to the clients, **leaving all the digital emails and texts behind**, we will never fully engage, build relationships, or create long-lasting sales opportunities. Without *reach*, we will fail.

In this diagram, I want you to focus on your identified top *A*-level category from the work earlier. Let's work on how we are going to sales attack our category As, and then you will really see this sales strategy coming together. As an example, here is one of mine!

Chapter 5

Target Clients

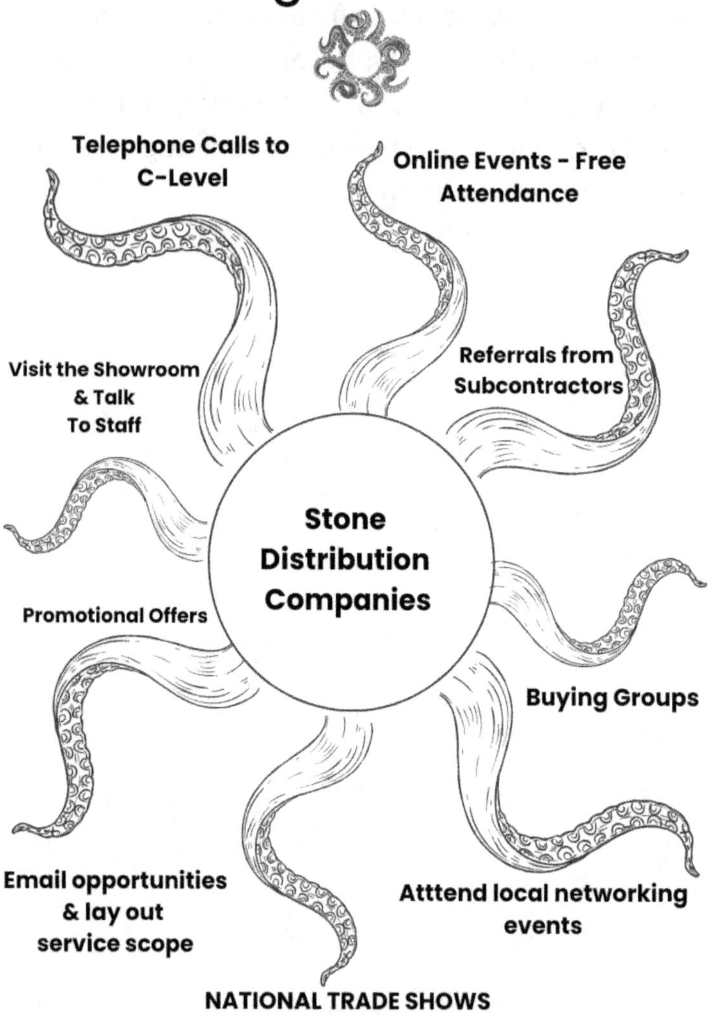

- Telephone Calls to C-Level
- Online Events - Free Attendance
- Visit the Showroom & Talk To Staff
- Referrals from Subcontractors
- **Stone Distribution Companies**
- Promotional Offers
- Buying Groups
- Email opportunities & lay out service scope
- Atttend local networking events
- NATIONAL TRADE SHOWS

Managing Marketing Time and Resources

With a well-defined target market in mind, you can allocate your resources and time effectively to the channels that will yield the best results. Don't you feel better already having identified who, when, how, and where you will reach your best and most profit-bearing customers? Managing marketing encompasses more than just social media platforms. Marketing efforts can take various forms, including in-person interactions or digital strategies. You've identified a few ways you will begin to market your business and sell your services by doing the diagrams above. While both in-person and digital techniques are effective in fostering business development, you must allocate time to thoroughly analyze each of your categories and determine the most effective strategy for each one. It is essential to acknowledge that not all methods work universally, and assuming otherwise would be a prime example of squandering valuable resources. Safeguarding your valuable resources, such as time, money, and energy, should be a top priority.

Time-management strategies

Later in chapter 12, I'll teach you how to strategize your time management and performance techniques. It's one of the most popular solution-based conversations in my programming. I'll even provide real-time tech resources that will save you time and money. For this chapter, just focus on how much time you will save once absorbing the weaknesses in your reactive strategies and what happens when you aren't focusing on the right clients.

When precise target marketing is in play, we take back our precious time. Use the exercise below to help you define areas of weakness in the selling strategy. You may begin to identify and clarify where you should be spending more of your precious time. And if you are lucky, you can hire someone to help accomplish these efforts.

Using a diagram method, formulate how much time it is *worth* spending on specific tasks and sales or marketing needs. Lauren Bowling writes in her Financial Best Life blog, "For me, knowing how much one hour of my time is worth helps me in everyday decisions both big and small, and it helps me balance all the different things on my plate: a baby, a new business, freelance clients, this website, and everything in between."[25] I agree with Lauren's thoughts here: it's precisely what a small business owner needs to hear! Please take a few minutes and decide what value you would place on your work per hour. The easy button formula goes like this:

What is your current annual revenue contribution divided by how many hours it took you to achieve the revenue, e.g., a month, quarter, or year? You will have to calculate how many hours are in that time frame in order to make the formula work.

> **Annual revenue/time expenditure in hours = $$$ / Hour**
>
> Or
>
> **Project revenue/time expenditure in hours = $$/Hour**

---

[25] Lauren Bowling, *Formula: When to Outsource and When to DIY,* Last updated May 13, 2023 –[https://financialbestlife.com/how-much-is-my-time-worth/]

Another way to look at it: What is the current hourly rate you charge a customer? Ensure you know your "worth" so you can allocate precious resources.

Once you know what an hour is worth to you, you can evaluate how you're spending your time. For example, evaluate if spending two hours in Canva designing a few Facebook posts is worth your time. For me it wasn't, as a professional can complete a video creative for Instagram in minutes, where it would take me hours.

Hiring a subcontracted sales manager to oversee and help your team might be more cost-effective than the time it takes you to spend a day (or several days) in a remote location. Outsourcing the accounting might be more cost-effective than managing that and selling.

So first, consider how much time you're spending marketing to each of your identified primary target categories, then apply the Pareto principle. How can we change the amount of time we spend on X to build better relationships with Y? Since you've evaluated the top performers and low revenue time sucks, applying and allocating time and resources will become clearer based on this formula.

Developing Intuition

So, at this point, you should be starting to build some **intuition** as to allocation of resources. Who, what, and how can we find the time to reach all these new prospects? **Intuition selling** is a big deal. In fact, it's my ultimate goal when training sales reps: helping them develop the natural process to identify leads, chase targets, and actualize sales. If you're going to use your *sales intuition* wisely, you will need to improve your sales engagement. We'll talk more about engagement in chapter 6, but for now, let's organize our process to outline this strategy and develop focus and clarity through a diagram.

Great, Alison, another f*^%% diagram! Listen, I get it, it's a lot of diagrams...but chances are you are a visual person too and charting out or outlining helps! That is why this works! If we are staring at computer screens and spreadsheets trying to unravel missed opportunities, we are blinded to the big picture. So, please bear with me and remember that keeping these diagrams in a notebook or on a corkboard will really help with those weeks when you are struggling to find your focus and just don't know where to begin. When you walk into the office some random Monday and don't know who to call or where to sell next, simply pull out the diagrams, and boom, a new beginning.

Resource allocation

The next step involves critically evaluating how you deploy your resources and determining the best avenues for investment based on your outlined strategies. Since we've already laid a solid foundation with our target persona and UVP and gauged our targeted market attack plan, we can now decide how much time = money and where we should spend it to create new business opportunities.

To figure it out, ask,

- What types of networking and sales efforts should I be hosting or participating in?
- Should I be going to more in-person events?
- Should I be attending more networking events?

- Based on the top categories, what kind of advertising dollars should I be throwing at participation in hosting or attending or sponsoring events?
- Should I be outsourcing help to take the marketing creative off my plate and placing it in the hands of a subcontractor?
- Should I be looking to hire part-time or full-time employees?

Remember the concept of attraction selling we discussed earlier? By really identifying the key money makers for your business, then using the diagrams to determine how you will reach them, you can align the target market with the most productive use of your resources. Before you begin, first decide what your budget will be for networking and marketing dollars annually.

According to Forbes.com, Thomas Minieri wrote, "If you want to maintain current revenue amounts, then five percent to ten percent of sales may suffice, however if you want rapid growth, then you may need to push that number higher...a startup business should commit to a fixed number for their advertising spend as their revenue maybe too low to follow the percentage of sales as a gauge. For many small businesses, $1,000 per month is a reasonable minimum advertising spend."[26]

So, in my case as an upstart, I chose a round number for my first year in business. $10,000 in marketing, networking, and advertising expenditures. This gave me a great beginning when considering my memberships to networking and industry

---

[26] "How Much Should You Spend on Marketing?" *Forbes*, April 13, 2022. https://www.forbes.com/councils/theyec/2022/04/13/how-much-should-you-spend-on-marketing/.

groups, sponsorship dollars for events, participation in conferences as well as any online advertising dollars. By the way, for my business, online advertising isn't a primary target at all! I know thanks to my target persona and brand strategy, presence is simply about keeping lines of communication open; thus, the real dollars I need to spend are on reaching my audience in person, which requires in-person events, participation in conferences, and the like.

Yours could look like radio ads, hiring a salesperson for outside, hiring a marketing person to keep up online engagement, etc. Hopefully, at this point from the first section of the book, and from our target marketing diagram exercises, the method of reach should be clear. Perhaps you need to hire that outside salesperson to spend more time cold- and warm-calling customers. Perhaps you need to hire that marketing company to help design mailers to reach the households you've identified as valuable. Perhaps you need to allocate money to that networking or buying group membership so you can get more exposure to larger groups of your customers. Perhaps you need to find the time to actually attend those meetings and do the in-person networking.

Now that you've assessed the needs to reach, and you know how much your time is worth, let's allocate resources available and find the time a little later.

I've done my category A for you to review and then formulate on your own. After splitting resource dollars, make sure you define your category A, category B, and then everyone else gets lumped into the leftover dollar amounts.

Try and follow along with these diagrams as examples. Keep applying that 80/20 formula whenever you are stuck on how to divide and don't forget to make notes about the resources you may need to acquire to succeed in reaching this category. You will notice, as I did, that with my smaller advertising budget, I simply can't afford to participate in large expensive events like exhibiting at trade shows. I had to come up with other ways to get noticed during my primary networking events and groups.

Doing this work will help you identify the same concept and avoid making large investment mistakes, not only with the wrong groups but in learning how to apply your best dollars to the best possible win for your business.

Chapter 5

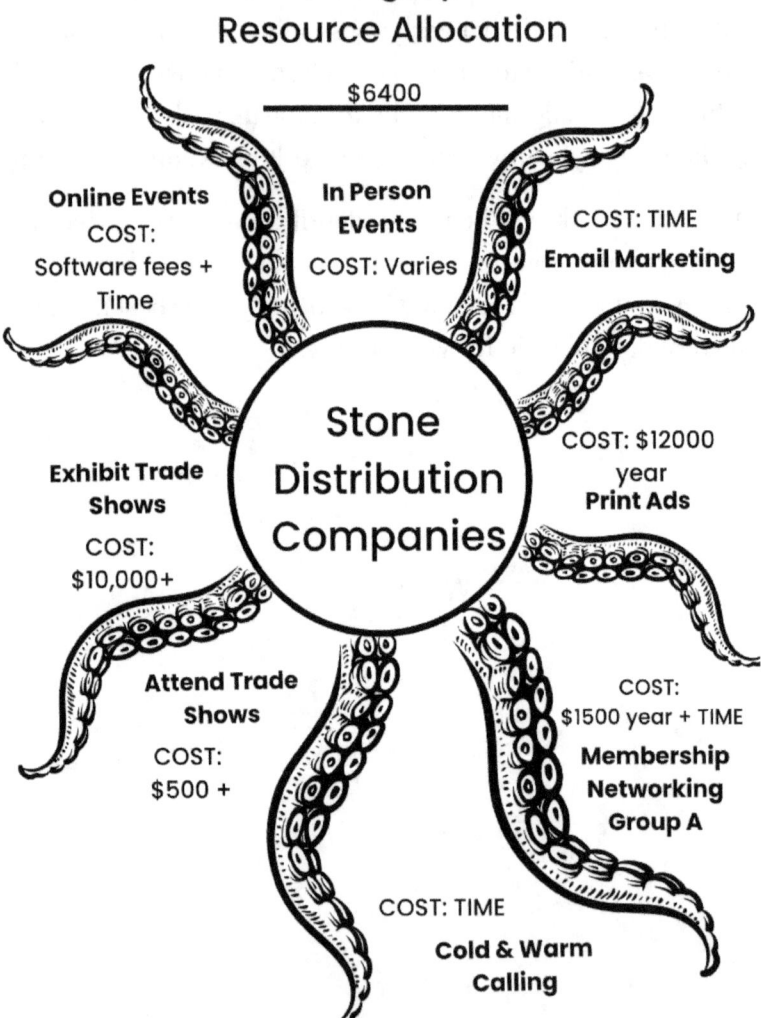

You will notice that it costs me very little time and energy to cold- and warm-call customers, email market, and attend in-person events. Also, if I identify a few key networking groups, my money can be spent on multiple memberships, fulfilling more opportunities for building speaking engagements and allowing for organic reach vs. paid reach. Because I am a smaller business, I can't afford the large ticket items like booths at trade shows. As my business grows, I will be able to expand my reach capability, and I will immediately have the intuition to know where best to put my advertising dollars. I'm so excited to help you learn this also because spending our hard-earned money is perhaps one of the biggest fears in business. We just don't want to make big mistakes in investing in our business' future.

I know I've given you a lot to consider. Now, let's look at the practical application of these techniques. This is a real client here in the USA. Names and locations have been changed to protect their privacy.

Chapter 5

Case Study: Northeast Mom & Pop B2B/B2C

To better explain the principles laid out previously, let me show you how this entire process worked to help find time and alleviate stress for one of my clients. Let me introduce you to Rebah and Geno T., a small mom-and-pop stone fabrication facility in the Northeast USA.

The situation

Rebah and her husband own a granite fabrication shop in Maine. With the exception of one part-time administrative employee who works a few hours during the week, Rebah and Geno run the business by themselves. Located over an hour and a half away from major metropolitan areas, they are often short on time. Geno works on installations or is at the back of the fabrication shop all day. Outside of the relationships he might develop while working in the field, his mind cannot be forward-facing toward sales. That leaves Rebah to deal with customer appointments, showroom management, accounting, administrative duties part-time, marketing and brand development, and prospective selling to bring in new business, both B2B and B2C. Sometimes, she spends two hours with a B2C client in the showroom, often leading to anxiety and frustration because the "other tasks" of the business get put on hold while she executes a lower-end sale. She must respond to client material changes, update quotes, and revise communication with distributors during the day. She also creates a huge time commitment to simple follow-up and proactive selling practices to please customers. Rebah is also responsible for procuring commercial opportunities and bidding digitally on projects. She wants to find time to complete more business relationships as they dream of continuing to develop a builder business, less consumer-driven installations, and they wish to service kitchen and bath companies who design the project so they can serve solely as a subcontractor, eliminating the time it takes to help consumers make product decisions. They need more employees to help, but they can't hire for a couple of reasons: they need more sales to afford the salesperson of their dreams, they can't afford the time to train someone new to the business, and even if they did hire an experienced salesperson (at a premium), they are spread too thin and want to drill down their optimal customer base.

Considerations

Part 1: Showroom Monopolizers—end the time suck. Customers categorized as Cs and Ds must be managed with careful timing observations and secure emotional intelligence. Rebah can monitor the body language of each walk-in and determine if she needs to set boundaries before they begin conversations. She can specify her next appointment and the period for meeting with the customer. Most importantly, if the buzzer is about to go off and she doesn't want to lose the client, she can set the next appointment before the customer leaves, meeting Maslow's hierarchy of needs and building a dedicated, safe, secure, and love-filled next session. Could she lose the customer? Based on the client category productivity rankings, this client doesn't fall in her 80 percent, so Rebah must be willing to reposition the client into a better time frame to buy from her. We already know this client isn't ready to sign today because otherwise, the client would be in full-decision mode. We are able to accomplish this by setting a follow-up appointment while the customer is still in the showroom and allowing this client to process some of the product options before returning for finalizing the order.

Part 2: Maximizing day trips & networking events. How does Rebah schedule time away from the office and create better relationship opportunities with co-op businesses? She likes attending at least one or two monthly events in larger cities. Rebah gets copies of RSVP lists from event hosts to identify attendees she wants to engage and create relationships with. Based on the same columns of information we worked on, she verified that she attended the correct events. With key companies like kitchen and bath showrooms and contractors or builders on the RSVP lists, Rebah can dedicate the day to getting appointments with these companies, leveraging the event to stop by for a product knowledge (PK) session or business offer. Making phone calls in advance to set one-on-one appointments makes her day more time-effective. Successful one-on-ones open more opportunities for warmer discussions during less work-related events and finding new contacts and referrals through these warm relationships.

Rebah can now outline the value of her time. After calculating her per hour worth, she also knows what her time means toward revenue. The client, industry, or appointment opportunity should be scheduled based on its priority on the ranking list. For instance, in Rebah's case, her profit margin and time to quote as well as time spent with a customer to make their decision all come into play when deciding her "hourly worth." We determined that while product categories do vary, Rebah's consultation time comes out to approximately $50 per hour. Now, Rebah is empowered to limit her time with specific customers—especially with customers where she has no room for profit margin at all. Rebah now recognizes when to hold, when to fold, and, above all, when to wrap up a conversation. Recognizing transactional benefits and learning to let go of loose ends maximizes efficiency while simplifying her plan for networking and combining it with outside sales time empowers better relationships and allows precious showroom time to cultivate her most profitable and desired business development targets. This comprehensive approach reassures Rebah about the effectiveness of the solutions and instills confidence in her ability to implement them successfully.

Customer analysis

Let's take Rebah's ideal prospect list, for instance. Rebah pulled her existing client list from her accounting software, she began by pulling the data into excel.

A. Low-hanging fruit. (B2B) Builders who communicate with quotes and expectations and negotiate time and money to close the deal: simple transactions and the best fit for their time management.

B. Cash cow. (B2B) Kitchen and bath showrooms with designer staff working directly for consumers. Rebah becomes the installer, not the customer service business, with very little final client interaction until the template.

C. Rock solid blue chips. (B2C) Contractor referrals—relationships already exist; they get appointments from contractor friends who are ready for this stage.

D. Repeat offenders. (B2C) Wholesaler referrals—Stoneyards refers clients to talk to them for fabrication and installation based on selecting materials in "whole" form at the wholesaler showroom.

E. Value Seekers/Skeptics. (B2C) Walk-in homeowners—people who found her on Google and walked in without an appointment and with few plans for their project. They are simply "shopping around."

Rebah found it fascinating that her preference for a business model was B2B instead of B2C, which she had initially assumed. She had not viewed their business as primarily focused on business-to-business interactions, so she had never thought of her target marketing in that way. I was thrilled to witness such a profound resolution.

Rebah identified "builders" as the ideal revenue stream for their small business and her primary target. Her small business doesn't have a perfect showroom for entertaining high-end consumers or catering to interior designers. That's also why their cash cow customers are kitchen and bath dealers within house designer staff. Rebah can but doesn't aspire to be a designer. This husband-and-wife team wants to remain behind the scenes, quoting dealers with in-house designers who must include the countertop or bath vanity as part of the overall project. It's important to remember that these categories can and will change as a business grows. It's important to remember that we never turn away from business theoretically, but we categorize for our ideals! We must recognize as business owners what we can realistically manage and what revenue we are "built" to manage.

Rebah's ideal subsegments are remodelers and higher-end kitchen and bath dealers because those companies typically handhold the consumer through their remodel process, and they need quotes, negotiation, template dates, and install dates from Rebah. Otherwise, far from the larger cities, her company is optional to participate in much of the selection process. They ideally want to serve as installers for service-oriented businesses only, not designing kitchens for the homeowners. Evaluating, we find this family business ideal target marketing business-to-business, not business-to-consumer. They need to focus on that B2B more than anything to keep the orders coming in from the "right" places.

Rebah needs to focus her **marketing** (read sales efforts) on builders, kitchen and bath dealers, and customers in her prioritization octopus (A, B, and C). She can also include the others. For example, see this pie chart of how the business might consider splitting their time and advertising dollars and allocating resources toward their business targets. Eighty percent of Rebah's business (and she wants it to) comes from the first three categories on the pie chart.

Chapter 5

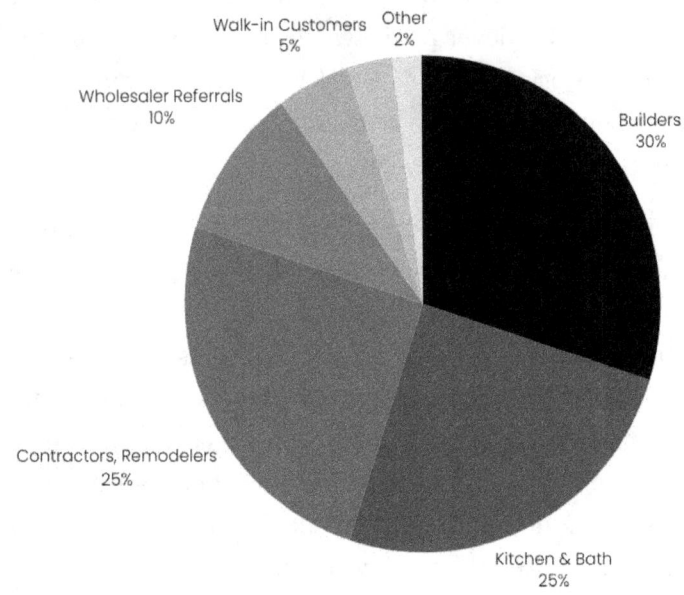

Isn't it amazing to see how much 80 percent of our business really is? How does this example pie chart collectively match our current revenue streams? While this perspective presents an idealistic vision of revenue generation, it is important to acknowledge that it may not always align with reality. The way we achieve our goals is through target marketing. Having established a foundational approach with a primary diagram, demographics are how we have traditionally guided our marketing and sales strategies. The basics of our customers: age, location, sex, marital status, for example. Often, we might fail to capture the nuances of our target's behavior. We need to understand what motivates our clients if we expect to lure them in with our tentacles. Let me show you how to attract the clients you want with more psychographic input.

Remember, psychographics moves us beyond mere statistics to explore psychological attributes including lifestyles, interests, attitudes, and values. For example, understanding that builders in our target market prioritize efficiency and reliability over cost can transform how we approach these relationships. Similarly, knowing that kitchen and bath showrooms value innovative design and exclusivity can help us position our offerings more effectively.

In Rebah's case, we can work on asset creation and implementation of her time and marketing strategy, which will keep her A, B, C target requirements continually engaged and flourishing repeat business. Following her 80 percent categories, we need to create:

- Tailored Account Time Management
- Focused Marketing Efforts
- Targeted Networking Groups
- Educational Workshops & Event Planning
- Loyalty Program Development

First, consider how much time you're spending on your categories. Think respectively about the hours you have available, as we've discussed in previous chapters, and apply the Pareto principle to this target marketing list. How can you change the amount of time you're spending on X to build better relationships with Y? Let's look at a few example scenarios from my area of expertise.

Psychographics to consider:

- Professional Goals & Aspirations
- Values & Attitudes
- Lifestyles & Interests
- Challenges & Pain points

Chapter 5

Rebah's Builders

Professional goals and aspirations. Builders focus on efficiency, reliability, and cost-effectiveness. They value partnerships that offer them streamlined solutions and dependable materials that won't delay their schedules. They often seek innovative building solutions that give them a competitive edge in bids and proposals.

Values and attitudes. Sustainability and durability of materials are increasingly important as more clients demand eco-friendly building options. Quality and craftsmanship are highly valued, as these directly affect their reputation.

Lifestyle and interests. Builders are keen on the latest construction technologies and trends. They might engage with content demonstrating thought leadership in construction management, efficient building techniques, or regulatory compliance.

Challenges and pain points. They are concerned with managing project timelines, sourcing dependable subcontractors, staying within budget—regulatory changes, and staying compliant with new building codes and safety standards.

Rebah's Kitchen and Bath Design Firms

Professional goals and aspirations. Designers need to stay at the forefront of design trends and innovations, providing clients with modern and stylish solutions. They often anchor toward brands synonymous with luxury, custom solutions, and creative design.

Values and attitudes. They value aesthetics, personalized design, client satisfaction, and relationships with suppliers who can provide unique, high-quality materials that cater to upscale client tastes.

Lifestyle and interests. Interested in design trends, architecture, and interior design magazines and exhibitions, they frequently seek inspiration from global design influences and successful design influencers on social media.

Challenges and pain points. They struggle with differentiation from competition and managing client expectations with realistic project scopes and budgets. They may have a hard time keeping up with design trends and source materials that meet design and functional quality standards.

Solutions

- ☐ **Outreach.** She should allocate her time to sales calls, follow-up, and focus offer emails and appointments on A, B, and C customer bases only. She is a one-person show and has little time to spend on outreach and business development, so the only categories Rebah needs to work on are her top three.
- ☐ **Personalized communication.** Keep these clients abreast of new materials available, new equipment, techniques, or new industry standards.
- ☐ **Social media.** For the builders, contractors, and remodelers, she should spend time on related platforms like LinkedIn and Facebook. Her Instagram and TikTok can cater to the kitchen and bath design firms.

Engagement programing.

- ☐ Create workshops and webinars geared toward each segment.
- ☐ Network in specific groups and events.

Does your business follow some similar clientele to Rebah's? Can you use this example to apply the psychographics to your customer base? Before we go, I'll leave another summary of step-by-step directions for creating those targeted segments and individualized marketing, i.e., how we are going to get sales plans.

Key takeaways—Action steps for the reader

Create your master octopus:

- ☐ Start with creating that master octopus master diagram and use the center circle to outline what you sell today.
- ☐ Write in any extras like a snippet of the UVP or target persona.
- ☐ Identify the "arms" of business segments you sell to.
- ☐ Start new diagrams for each arm when you want to dive deeper into a category.

Create your prioritization chart—remember those categories! Time to rank our priority clients.

- ☐ Highest-value customers with efficient current revenue
- ☐ Second-tier or aspirational customers, outlining what business we want more of
- ☐ Lowest valuation of clients, or the business we don't want at all
- ☐ Remember, you don't have to work as hard for customers with established relationships to maintain. You must serve lower-priority customers, but they must be a more significant piece of the pie.

Create your tailored target market *reach* octopus diagram

- ☐ Put the "ideal" business segment or client in the center.

- ☐ Add networking groups possible for interaction.
- ☐ Add any preferred social media channels.
- ☐ Add areas of events or education channels of interest.
- ☐ Add loyalty program ideas of interest.
- ☐ Write the ranking at the top or bottom.
- ☐ Define any other methods based on your data from section one on how you might best reach these clients.

Allocate resources from your advertising budget

- ☐ Use the 80/20 principle to divide your marketing and advertising sales budget based on level A category first.
- ☐ Define costs for reach and apply them to each octopus arm, visualizing the expense.
- ☐ Formulate decisions on reach and financial objectives required.
- ☐ Follow the process for category B and all other categories identified.

By following these guidelines, individuals in various roles, such as key account managers, inside salespeople, outside salespeople, entrepreneurs, product developers, manufacturers, wholesalers, and anyone else, can completely transform their approach to selling. The key is to sell smarter, not harder. Prioritize, identify, and create a strategy to spend your time and money wisely. Crack down on a new focus and stop *squirreling* where you don't belong.

Boom! You now have a formulated plan of attack for every arm of opportunity! Doesn't it feel good? Has the fog lifted? Are you excited to get going? That's the typical experience with my clients when we get to this point. So, get ready to rumble and get ready to sell!

CHAPTER 6

Mastering Engagement

Rethink Business Relationships & Attraction Selling

In this chapter we're going to discuss how to effectively "work the room" and find ways to sell without having to stand in front of someone and pitch our hearts out. By crafting diagrams and charts in the last chapter, you should now have a much clearer picture of precisely who you need to be targeting, and you've got some ideas for branching out and creating new relationships either B2B or B2C. I'm pretty sure you've also identified a few budget changes and resources needed to take action towards **proactive attraction selling**.

With foundations in place, let's define the *how* even more! It's time to **master customer engagement**—focusing on how we connect, and stay connected with our target network, all the while **creating opportunities for sales and referrals**.

Chapter 6

Engagement can be defined in different ways. Merriam-Webster states it is "the state of being in gear."[27] At the same time, the University of Oxford defines business engagement as "the development of mutually beneficial partnerships between academic researchers and industry to address real-world challenges."[28] It's interesting to see the correlation between these two definitions! Both definitions correlate engagement with solving problems; I especially like the idea of being "in gear," as it sets a **tone of action.** Forbes describes customer engagement as something that "involves building relationships with customers at every touch point. It involves understanding customer needs, preferences, and pain points. It's about tailoring brand-related experiences to meet and exceed those expectations."[29] Remember like I pointed out in chapter five, we have to create touch points with our customers or we will fail in business.

B2B & B2C Engagement Concepts:

- Customer loyalty programs
- Personalized outreach = offers, phone calls, email & texting
- Harnessing feedback
- Onsite and offsite events

Whether B2B or B2C, sales professionals must continually focus on nurturing relationships, which means staying engaged even after the sale to maintain long-term relationships.

---

[27] "Engage," Merriam-Webster, accessed August 20, 2024, https://www.merriam-webster.com/dictionary/engage.
[28] "Engagement," University of Oxford, accessed August 20, 2024, https://www.oxford.ac.uk/engagement.
[29] "Understanding Customer Engagement," Forbes, accessed August 20, 2024, https://www.forbes.com/customer-engagement.

BEYOND ORDER MAKERS

Customer loyalty programs

Albemarle Countertop Co., a long-time client, became a top sales leader thanks to a manager's suggestion to roll out an exclusive rebate program. The idea was to keep a client engaged for all four quarters in a year and provide a percentage rebate during the first quarter of the following year. Since rebates are based upon previous sales, it makes it easy for businesses to hold back percentages of sales in order to pay out the rebate in the allotted time frame. We formulated based on a percentage increase over last year's sales. For example, if we sold the client $100,000 in materials in 2020, we would like to see a 25 percent increase in sales for 2021. Whatever total net sales the customer ended up purchasing over the last year, we would provide a 5-10 percent rebate scaled accordingly. So, at the end of 2021, if the client increased their purchases to $150,000, meaning their new net sales was $250,000, they would receive a rebate of anywhere between $1,250 and $2,500. As a business, you can apply the rebate as a credit on someone's account, or if possible, send them an actual check, which can be applied as they see fit. As their salesperson, over the course of the year, it was my job to keep their loyalty program tally running and remind them quarterly where we stand on the approximate rebate. The process worked so well that we could onboard five of our top clients with this reward system, keeping their purchasing loyalty focused on our brand, not the competition.

> ***Pro tip!*** *Remember rebates are based on net sales, not gross. Be careful promising rebate totals to clients.*

Chapter 6

B2B Customer Loyalty Ideas

Rebate programs. As mentioned above, they are structured based on solid profit margins and pricing structures that do not cut too far into the bottom line and encourage longevity in business relationships.

Volume discounts. The more they buy, the deeper the discount. Provide percentage discounts based on volume.

Early pay discounts. If an invoice is paid within thirty days, offer a 5–10 percent discount on the total. This will keep the client interested in paying early or on time.

Product exclusivities. Group a section of clients and form a relationship for exclusivity in new product launches. Only this group can access the newer line of materials over specific periods.

Contract renewal incentives or loyalty discounts. Similar to the Rebate program, reward loyalty to returning customers. The discount can be as little as 5 percent, and customers will often return for the savings.

Annual education trip discounts. If an industry group takes a trip annually, you could sponsor a portion of the cost of that trip. Given how much airfare is rising, would offering $100 or $200 toward the cost of airfare be tempting for a client?

Free education seminars. Offer exclusive education opportunities on the business's dime. It's an opportunity to build a networking event and loyalty simultaneously. We'll talk more about customizing events a little later in this chapter.

B2C Loyalty Program Ideas

Point-based rewards systems. A popular program for food and beverage, a point system could easily be applied to any retail establishment, encouraging customers to return and keep an ongoing rewards system. Credit cards are wildly successful with these systems and promote cash back for point exchange. This can apply to almost any product or service-based business, especially when repeat visits are a requirement in your business plan.

Subscription services. This type of loyalty program works wonders with B2C service-based businesses. Doesn't everyone want $20 a month from thousands of customers? A carefully thought-out annual or monthly membership with discounts on goods and services is all the rage in 2024. Some considerations for creating subscriptions:

- Use tiered structures to entice levels and create more availability toward varied customer income levels
- Be flexible with cancellations and make sure to have written policies for refunds
- Consider creating the easiest possible methods for sign-up and renewals
- Make sure you have enough added value for a monthly or annual membership

Surprises. Remember the free dessert from Panera Bread for your birthday? Occasionally surprising loyal customers with unexpected benefits, such as free products, upgrades, or handwritten thank-you notes, creates a heartwarming experience. Birthday or holiday freebies are one way of giving a gift or discount and showing that we remember the special days in people's lives.

Social media & member badges. Reward customers for engaging with a brand by sharing posts, writing reviews, or participating in online contests. These systems can increase brand visibility and foster a sense of community.

Personalized outreach

How many emails do you delete each day? Take a quick peek at your deleted email box from last week and count. Just look at some of these current email statistics. Courtesy of Forbes Advisor[30] and Porch Group Media:[31]

- "Consumers spend an average of ten seconds reading branded emails."
- "74 % of people hate being shown irrelevant content, which makes personalization incredibly important to a successful email marketing strategy."
- "Emails that are personalized increase open rates by 26%."
- "Personalized emails are six times more likely to drive conversions."
- "Emails with the recipient's name in the subject line have an eighteen percent open rate."
- "Those that do not have names in the subject line only have a fifteen percent open rate."
- "Including the word 'free' in the subject line was ten percent more successful in being opened."
- "Forty-two percent of users delete emails that are not optimized for mobile devices."

---

[30] "Email Marketing Statistics 2024," *Forbes Advisor*, accessed August 15, 2024, https://www.forbesadvisor.com/email-marketing-statistics-2024/.
[31] "Mobile Optimization and Email Engagement," Porch Group Media, accessed August 15, 2024, https://www.porchgroupmedia.com/mobile-optimization-email/.

- "The best days for emails are Tuesday and Thursday."
- "11:00 AM is the best time for sending emails, and midnight shows the highest CTR."
- "The worst open and click-through rates are on weekends."
- "Email open rates are consistent throughout the week, with Saturday marginally taking the top spot at 37 percent."
- "In B2B: 77 percent of B2B buyers say their preferred form of contact is email."
- "In B2C: The average abandoned cart email open rate is 50 percent, a 15 percent increase on the average email marketing open rate."
- "Forty-seven percent of email marketers surveyed said they use AI when creating their email marketing campaigns."

The delete-before-reading rate has increased rapidly in the last eight years and is increasingly rising.

- "2015, the delete before reading rate was 9 percent."[32]
- "2016, marketing profs reported it increased to 13 percent."[33]
- "2018, this number increased to 18 percent."[34]

---

[32] "Email Open and Delete Rates, 2015-2020," MarketingCharts, accessed August 19, 2024, https://www.marketingcharts.com/industries/government-and-politics-65987.

[33] "Email Statistics Report, 2015-2020," Marketing Profs, last modified 2020, https://www.marketingprofs.com/email-statistics-report.

[34] "Consumers don't mind deleting emails before reading," Digital Commerce 360, last modified April 25, 2019, https://www.digitalcommerce360.com/2019/04/25/consumers-dont-mind-deleting-emails-before-reading/

- "2020, the number has reportedly increased to 35 percent."[35]
- According to the Nielsen Norman Group, a leader in user experience data, in 2024, "68 percent of emails [weren't] even opened."[36]

Customized offers

Based on these statistics, you can see the relevance of customizing our email approach; for me, less is more. Did you also notice some inconsistencies in my quote sources? Yes, sometimes Saturday night, sometimes midnight on Friday. Everyone is different, and every business needs to consider how much is too much and find that sweet spot for their clientele. You need to ask, "What is appropriate for my clients?" As we will discuss later, I found collecting feedback about my efforts personally and consistently over a year extremely helpful to ensure I was staying on track. For my Grassi Pietre builder clients, I have found that many responses and read rates increase on Sunday evenings. For my Rep Methods clients, I have had the greatest success sending blogs early on Saturday mornings. Thankfully my web service has a tracking program as most email systems do, allowing me to evaluate the success of each campaign. Don't waste these free resources with our paid providers; analytics are important. Try a few of these expert suggestions and see what works for your business.

A little more advice: Whatever you do, don't use that BCC element and mass email the whole group, despite how easy it is.

---

[35] "35% of Emails Are left unread: A Data-Driven Analysis," getmailbird.com, accessed August 19, 2024, https://www.getmailbird.com/email-use-statistics/
[36] "Email User Experience," Nielsen Norman Group, accessed August 20, 2024, https://www.nngroup.com/reports/email-user-experience.

We've all been there: tasked with emailing a contact list of two hundred people and looking for a quick way to get this over with, we copy and paste all the contact emails into the BCC field on the email and hit send.

Guilty! Oh boy, am I guilty! It just doesn't work. Spam filters pick up on this now, and it's pretty much a useless tactic.

Create distribution lists. The best practice here is to consider grouping a few clients with those fantastic categories we discovered in prioritization. Another option is to group clients with specific buying preferences or design aesthetics. Did you know that most email programs have the ability to create groups quickly and easily? Distribution groups help us target the right customers with the right message. Organizing our email lists into smaller segments makes our daily, weekly, or monthly communication requirements more manageable and faster! We may have to audit or update periodically, but for the general day to day, we have these custom lists ready to go and can send personalized emails to the right audience at the right time. Personalization and customized communication win every. single. time.

For example, one of my clients has an internal marketing team that creates monthly newsletters for the entire customer base over four locations. We know there is value in what the marketing department has spent hours of dedicated time creating, but for an even more significant effect, they could use that beautiful document and send customized versions to each client category. Could your mail software make an A/B version of a marketing email?

Chapter 6

Please don't overdo it. Did you notice those "deleted before reading" statistics? I delete everything from my inbox if it's a promotional email from a retailer online. I also go on unsubscribe binges occasionally because of all the clutter! Take a cue from your habits and consider what will appeal to the audience before crafting and hitting send.

Phone calls. And what about phone calls? Noting the stats about email marketing, isn't it time we consider picking up the phone again? Listen, I'm in my mid-forties and falling in between the ancient generation of pre-internet and the new generations of people who can't live without the handheld computer device we call a phone, so I know I'm biased toward the effectiveness of a traditional phone conversation. But let me tell you a story about a twenty-something and her light bulb about phone conversations, effectiveness, and time management.

Sweet Theresa manages a showroom in Texas and is relatively new to the industry and sales! Her brain is thriving when it comes to customization and client personalization. However, she came to me struggling with the time it takes to craft these personal offers and invitations weekly. She is also working to get responses to her email requests for project information before showroom appointments. During one of our coaching calls, I asked her to consider picking up the phone and how much time it might save her. Could she call the client in the morning? What about twenty-four hours ahead? What if she could cut through all the delay and happenstance of waiting for a reply and pick up the phone? I could have cried with the look of excitement and "ah-ha" moment that flashed across her face! Yes, she exclaimed, "I get it. Yes, I could make five phone calls faster than ever and send five crafted emails." That conversation would provide connection, question and answer, feedback, inspiration, creativity, and suggestions toward her selling tactics, all wrapped up in a ten-minute conversation. I challenge any Gen X or Gen Y who might pick up this book to consider getting off the email and onto a conversation.

Texting. Texting is genius. It's literally changed the way our society communicates. But is it meant for conversations? NO! It is meant for conversation starters. I love sending a photo or a question via text, and the client responds with a phone call. It's literal attention-grabbing magic. The beauty of texting is we have a record of those conversations we can turn to later for follow-up.

What about bulk texting to client databases? According to Constant Contact, "Open rates are as high as 98 percent."[37]

What if we forwarded a crafted bulk message to a handful of our contacts, specifically mentioning a product they intended to purchase already?

Will the client respond to the mass marketing item or the personalized text? Think carefully before investing in fancy software. Spam filters are getting smarter and wiser! The more we try to "mass text," the more we end up in the unread zone. According to TextRequest.com's article "How Do Carriers Identify Spam Texting?," carriers look for things that would be harmful to their customers or unwanted. The eight triggers

---

[37] "Email User Experience," Nielsen Norman Group, accessed August 20, 2024, https://www.nngroup.com/reports/email-user-experience.

below are common in what carriers have confirmed as spam texts: [38]

- Free or unbranded shortened links
- When links are placed at the end of the message
- Avoid using naked links
- Messages including words in ALL CAPS
- Messages with special characters
- Multiple identical messages
- Long messages
- Robotic, misspelled, or grammatically incorrect sentences

Create distribution lists. Just like with emails, texting personalization wins every time. Consider cutting your contact list into labels or groups and creating small lists catered for a handful of customers. Suggestions for labels or lists: Networking group name, previous purchase(s), category of style or design choice, geographic location, product affiliation, industry group . . . to name a few.

Hosting onsite or offsite events

Exclusivity, the all-important ego stimulator! If we can build feelings of exclusivity with our customers, we begin building the community that fosters our relationships. One way to build community is through events, which encourages the loyalty factor we discussed earlier in chapter four. Events are one of my pride and joys in selling and business development. People like coming together for the most part, and if we can invite them to something exclusive and educational, our clients feel

---

[38] "How Do Carriers Identify Spam Texting?" TextRequest, accessed August 19, 2024, https://www.textrequest.com/insights/avoid-texts-marked-as-spam.

special. It doesn't have to cost thousands of dollars. To make events feel exclusive, spend a little money on the invitation portion and don't just do events or email blasts to curate a message to a specific audience. Also, the smaller the event, the more focused the clientele, and the less expensive the process. Often, I encourage clients to have an event monthly—yes, monthly! It doesn't have to be a blowout. Still, something curated and trimmed for a specific group of customers who get along, do business with each other, belong to a specific networking group, or introduce a new neighbor to the experienced network. It's impressive how forward-facing events and personalized interactions foster the best relationships. If this all feels like too much work, ask for help or another friendly business to co-op or trade months with you! It's like BOGO for business relationships.

A quick story before I move on: A client of mine owns a paint store and is struggling to get clients in the door. She would host events, and no one would show. She would spend hours preparing the food and decorations and spend zero time ensuring she had a guest list and confirmations. I mentioned co-oping with a local real estate brokerage firm. The broker would entertain any existing clients for the firm at the showroom; in exchange, the paint shop owner could attend those events whenever there was an open house, providing free paint advice to any potential buyers. A win for both groups and a momentous success, a partnership quickly formed, and the mutual referral helped both ladies gain new client leads and regular exposure to the end-user customer.

Harnessing feedback

The most straightforward approach is leveraging surveys and feedback forms on our websites. Integrating automation and contact us forms within your digital presence is simple. Consider setting up automation to trigger weeks after a transaction. While seeking immediate feedback post-sale is common, it can sometimes be more insightful to allow customers time to reflect on their experience. Think about how and when you would prefer to be approached for feedback. If you need more clarification, conduct a few tests to determine the most effective timing. Online services like Acuity, Mailchimp, or Trustpilot can facilitate this process for small businesses. I use Wix for my website services, which offers a selection of pre-designed templates for automation and customizable feedback collection. Google Forms is also a handy, free tool for creating tailored questionnaires and embedding them on your site as needed.

Experience surveys, feedback forms, and questionnaires. After a recent team training, I received feedback via a form from both industry veterans and younger team players. The reviews came through positive and some mixed results. What I initially took away as negative feedback, I could use as a learning opportunity. Instead of viewing the not-so-positive reviews as a setback, I saw it as a chance to refine my approach to include pre-workshop activities that aligned with participant mindsets. This adaptation ensures that all attendees are on board, enhancing effectiveness.

Arranging in-person customer interviews can effectively manage business-to-business (B2B) feedback. As we continually seek ways to engage with our business clients, offering to meet over a coffee or a light snack for a candid discussion about their experiences or recent transactions shows a deep commitment to understanding and meeting their needs. This personal touch demonstrates that you value their input and cements your relationship by showing your willingness to adapt to better serve them.

But what about business-to-consumer (B2C) feedback? The dynamics differ significantly. While gathering B2C feedback for continuous improvement is crucial, the approach is similar to B2B. However, we can revive "old school" tactics like sending thank-you notes or small appreciation gifts, which can significantly impact us. Consider including a small incentive that matches their interests or preferences when asking for their feedback. For instance, a gift card to a retailer they favor can be a successful touch—as it aligns with their likes and dislikes. Whether they're wine aficionados, avoid certain mega-stores, or aren't coffee enthusiasts, tailoring your thank-you can dramatically increase engagement and provide the feedback necessary to refine your offerings.

Hosting events and gathering feedback. How about using an event to gather feedback? Leveraging personalized events to gather data can be an incredibly effective strategy for understanding your client's needs and preferences more deeply. As I stated earlier, I encourage clients to host and attend events; it's not just about networking—it's about seizing every opportunity to gain insights that can drive your business forward. Personalized events provide a unique platform to engage with peers and clients in a relaxed, informal setting, which can lead to more candid and insightful feedback.

Personalized events, such as workshops, seminars, or casual meetups, offer a perfect backdrop for meaningful conversations. These events allow you to display your brand's personality, foster more robust connections, and create a sense of community. More importantly, personalized events present an opportunity to gather qualitative data captured through surveys or digital interactions.

Incorporate some of these ideas into your next event to harness those customer insights and boost the networking opportunity:

- Interactive workshops and breakout sessions. Organize interactive workshops and breakout sessions where participants can discuss specific topics related to your business. Use these sessions to pose questions and gather feedback on your products or services. Facilitators can take notes and engage participants in discussions that reveal valuable insights.
- Feedback stations. Set up dedicated stations or booths where attendees can provide feedback. Try suggestion boxes, digital kiosks, or even staffed tables where team members can engage with guests and record their thoughts and suggestions.
- Live polls and Q&A sessions. During presentations or panel discussions, use live polling tools to gather real-time feedback from attendees. Polls engage your audience and provide immediate insights into their preferences and opinions. A group in Chicago did this during one of my live classes, and participation increased even though many participants dialed in from remote locations.

▸ Post-event surveys. Send surveys immediately after the event to capture attendees' fresh impressions. Make the study concise and relevant to the event's content. Offering a small incentive, like a discount or entry into a raffle, can increase response rates. Or don't wait to close the event or let attendees leave without completing a survey on the spot!

Harnessing feedback at someone else's event. You can even get feedback at someone else's event.

☐ Asking open-ended questions: Engage in conversations that go beyond small talk. Ask open-ended questions about industry trends, challenges your peers and clients face, and their expectations from businesses like yours.

☐ Observe and listen: Pay attention to recurring themes and concerns in discussions. These can provide clues about areas where your business can improve or innovate.

☐ Ask for follow-up: During the event, implore customer interviews. Ask the attendees when and how you can follow up with them! Allowing participants to explain how and when increases the probability of a response.

☐ Social media listening: We covered this during the social media conversation in the book's first section. Taking the time to implore conversations on other group networks and participating in discussions is a successful way to harness feedback about your business and those of different performers in your market or industry.

Building Long-Term Relationship Ideas

Engagement and effective communication are the building blocks of relationships, but it's your ability to sustain these interactions over time that leads to lasting success.

Cross-merchandise your brand with other businesses and, above all, build strong, personalized communication strategies to elevate our value.

- **Identify key partnerships** in the business sector, known or perceived (these partnerships will help us formulate our *how*)
- **Identify complementary products or services**
- **Identify shared values and brand identities**
- **Determine reach and influence**

Ultimately, mastering customer relationships demands a strategic and empathetic approach that incorporates the principles of trust, tailored communication, and proactive service. It requires a commitment to delivering consistent value and building trust and loyalty through transparency, personalization, and ongoing engagement. By embracing these principles, sales professionals can differentiate their brand in a crowded marketplace and cultivate a loyal customer base that will contribute to long-term success.

As a small business, I identify with frugality and what it means to get creative with my brand merchandising to increase the probability of making a profit by creating minimal overhead, subcontractor acquisition, or expensive advertising plans. When I started Rep Methods, I could only avoid debt by using my savings. As any small business startup goes, that savings turns into debt, and then gradually becomes revenue, and the debt becomes smaller until we decide to invest our profits and or borrow more to grow. It's an inevitable cycle of winning and investing and sometimes losing. It takes time. I had to grip this understanding, swallow it whole even when it painfully ached as it moved down my acceptance throat. When I realized that my almost nonexistent advertising budgets were too slim to start risking Google and social media ads, I had to get creative about strategic partnerships and bonds with other coaches and business consultants with whom I could pair my model. Only within those bonded relationships, built with trust and cooperative selling, could I grow. Slowly. I must admit the pill of time is a large one to swallow when you want to succeed by staying away from red numbers, and everything in your belly tells you it's just a matter of time. The truth is, despite the pain of being a young business, with patience, time, due diligence, and good target marketing planning, we do eventually crawl out of the debt hole and learn how to apply our earnings properly to reinvest in the business, so don't feel lost if my above description fits you too. That's why you're reading this book, aren't you? To get ahead of the potential demons of debt! Good job and keep going. Just like we identified in chapter 5: we can really get creative with low-budget ways of active selling when the belts are tight.

Cross-merchandising and strategic partnerships are a good way to low-budget cross sell for startups, entrepreneurs, and coaches alike. Larger businesses with more capital might also afford stronger bonds, and those with primary investments plus returns can afford to invest and capitalize on existing relationships. As a small entity, for this book, let's focus on the lower end, which is more cost-effective (i.e., closer to FREE options) in merchandising your brand with the help of strategic partnerships. Recognizing the significance of identifying partnerships and merchandising sales is a pivotal strategy for business growth.

Identify key partnerships

To align with another entity, choose partners whose target audiences overlap with yours but are not direct competitors. A collaborative campaign reaches a relevant audience for both parties. What does this look like? Think installers cross-merchandising with retailers or referral sources with whom you already have relationships.

Take, for instance, one of my private sales training clients specializing in construction drawings. (Names and locations have been changed.)

Case study

Julie has worked in the building industry for the last ten years and started a service-based business providing construction drawings for builders, designers, kitchen and bath retailers, and fabricator customers. While Julie initially began small as a sub and kept a full-time job, she eventually gained enough traction and wanted to become a full-time independent contractor.

When she wanted to grow her business, Julie found me through a mutual friend. She couldn't figure out how to sell her work and still do her job at the same time. We needed to work out some of her time-management conundrums while formulating a strategic business development plan, allowing her to concentrate on selling only briefly during the week. Her construction drawings and consultations take up most of her time, so she needed a quick-and-dirty resource plan to establish new relationships and sell her services for only a few hours each week.

First, we worked on the basic organization principles from my workshop, slowly helping her cut fat from her time issues while giving her confidence in forming better task lists and organizing her time into work blocks. Then, we went on to creating a full-blown selling strategy.

Successfully, the ideas came together on how she should align and begin selling her services to other companies in the area and begin to market herself with zero cost in advertising.

The simplest way for Julie to capture leads was to use her existing contact base. We started analyzing her existing relationships and breaking down the list of companies she had worked for in the past and developed a strategy to put her brand within this subcontractor segment independently. Once Julie started putting the puzzle pieces together with her work history and existing relationships in the stone fabrication world, she could align with these existing, functioning, and running businesses while capitalizing on their relationships! I loved watching the light bulb click on as she realized that by simply working on her existing relationships that run parallel to her business, she could ask for referrals directly, and work would start to pour in.

Chapter 6

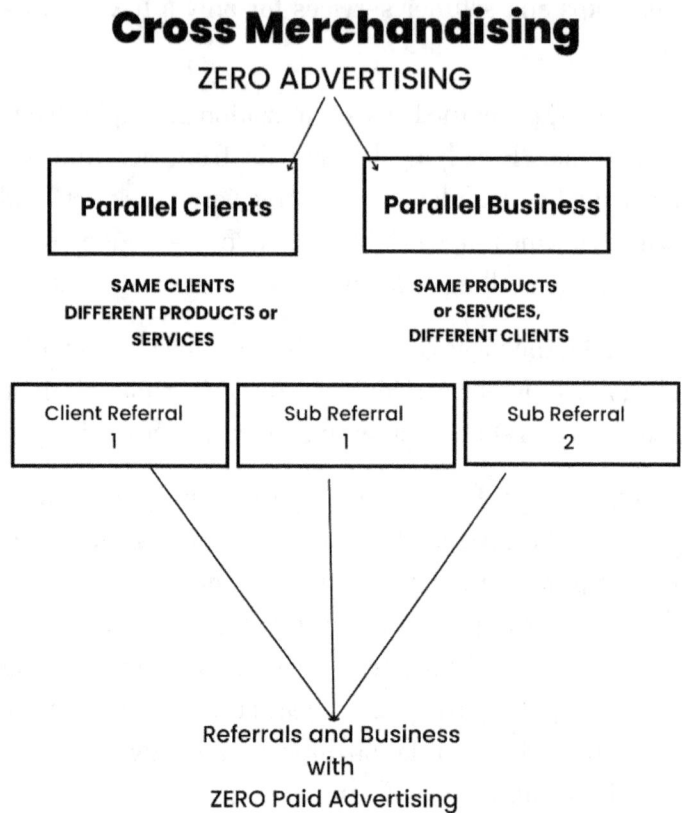

Ideally, we needed to merchandise Julie's brand and service with zero advertising dollars since she had no startup money and still worked full time. We knew that by simply creating quick engagements via phone, some in person, and as much as possible touches through client referrals, she wouldn't have to spend much time building social channels and creating content. In fact, because of the style of her business, she could keep a low-key offline presence and use those co-op partnerships to start saving for any future advertising in the next few years. Ideally, Julie wouldn't ever have to advertise in the general marketing sense; instead, she creates a flow of business exchange and works her network for more pieces of the builder and designer pie. This diagram should help you align a similar principle for your service or product business.

Complementary products or services

When forming partnerships for cross-promotional efforts, the logical choice often involves products or services that complement each other seamlessly. For example, in the kitchen and bath industry, it's common to see countertop and cabinet brands showcased together, targeting a shared demographic with similar price points.

Despite the seeming simplicity, successfully implementing cross-merchandising can be a challenge. This is particularly relevant for B2B sales reps who require other companies with complementary brands to help promote my product or service. I have firsthand experience with this challenge from my early career. Relying on others to promote our brand is risky since we can only control our own efforts and not the outcome.

Take, for instance, my experience representing a well-known countertop brand. Early on, the brand faced resistance within the luxury sector because of its association with large retail chains like Lowe's and Home Depot. Luxury retailers hesitated to engage in cross-merchandising efforts for fear of diluting their exclusivity factor.

Attempting to penetrate every market segment proved to be a misstep, resulting in wasted resources and a diluted brand image. Fortunately, I could pivot by focusing on selective distribution channels, preserving the brand's appeal by customizing the offering within those luxury dealerships.

Furthermore, trying to be universally seen in the market proved ineffective, leading to neglected display samples and diminished brand reputation. This experience taught me the importance of customizing my merchandising efforts, limiting broad outreach, emphasizing quality over quantity, and changing how we were viewed in various partnerships and distribution channels.

Shared values and brand identity

Collaborating with partners who share similar values and brand identity is not just essential, it's crucial. This approach not only strengthens the integrity of our brand but also enhances the resonance and impact of our collaborative efforts in the market.

Today, I approach cross-merchandising with a mindset akin to operating on borrowed time. I have learned to apply more filters for whom I pursue meetings with when I'm traveling for my client in Italy. When it comes to my sales coaching, I have learned that it is no use pursuing clients with five hundred employees and vast levels of sales teams and organization channels. They are simply too big for my customized hands-on approach. (I am only one person.) When I'm researching potential business partners, I typically look for those who share our intricate values. Working in certain markets, I don't want to place my luxury goods in the large and multifaceted wholesaler. I seek boutique, private, strategic partners with clients who are already searching for similar unique products. It doesn't make sense to place our brand where it will get lost. So, I typically use the "find the similar brand" approach, but also, I look for value in what the company doesn't offer just as much as brands they already market. This approach not only strengthens my products' integrity but also enhances the tone and impact of our collaborative efforts in the market.

As in Julie's case, which I referenced earlier, building long-term relationships with businesses or individuals you already have a positive relationship with can be a key to success. This approach may require patience but can foster trust and collaboration, leading to mutual growth and success.

The most effective way is to pinpoint businesses that display these qualities and are fit for a cooperative partnership with similar nuances.

Determining the reach and influence

By gauging the partner's reach and impact in their respective industry or community, the collaborative campaign can extend its reach by forming partnerships with influential entities.

For example, again, using my wholesaler search across the country, I wanted to partner with companies with target markets already in place. The passion for similar products must be there, and our client lists should be identical, preexisting, or following the same guidelines. I like to partner with businesses where the lead owner or salesperson has worked diligently to make a face within the community.

When partnering with service companies, it's helpful when we both already align with similar clientele! This is exactly like our story about Julie and formulating her cross-merchandising, free advertising plan.

Chapter 6

Conclusion

Mastering engagement is about understanding that selling isn't just about transactions but about creating lasting connections and building trust. In this chapter, we explored how to "work the room" by fostering loyalty, maintaining personalized outreach, gathering valuable feedback, and hosting engaging events. By doing so, you can turn one-time interactions into long-term relationships that generate ongoing opportunities for sales and referrals. Remember, true engagement is proactive, adaptive, and centered on genuinely understanding and connecting with your customers.

Now that you have a solid grasp of how to build and nurture relationships, the next step is to focus on refining your skills and knowledge to sustain and expand this growth. In the next chapter, we'll dive into training and professional development strategies that target specific business growth areas. From identifying skill gaps to leveraging outsourcing, we'll explore how to continuously improve and position yourself and your business for long-term success. Let's get started on crafting a strategic approach to ongoing growth and development.

CHAPTER 7
Training and Professional Development for Targeted Business Growth

Along the way, I've found remarkable allies who have joined me on this journey. Both established brands and businesses, as well as upstarts, have created online forums and brand communities. Interestingly, whenever I stumble upon a new prospect or receive any indication of a potential lead, the initial reaction from about 90 percent of my clients is to complain about needing more time to sell. Following complaints, many individuals admit to needing to be more knowledgeable about strategies to grow their client base and improve their contact lists. My friends, that is precisely why I'm here. You need to identify training needs and be aware of the types of training programs available for target marketing and business development, both internal and external.

You're here, reading this chapter, so you've inevitably recognized the need for help in this department, right? It's a relief. Congratulations! You've completed the first step toward change: admit that you need help! I laugh because over the years, I've worked with a few twelve-step programs in my life, all of which have been enormously beneficial in getting me to change, and it's the absolute truth; at first, we must admit some defeat and look for help. This step is the most difficult for a solopreneur.

Determine Your Training

Typically, if you work for a company, they offer training. Given that CRM systems are a heavy-duty culprit for a new hire, companies often have a trainer on staff who can show new hires how to manipulate the data to see how to follow up better.

If you're a solopreneur, you need to find your own trainer. Is there a trainer available on a simple hourly basis to help with specific tips and tricks about software, helping you save time and gather data faster?

But it isn't just the technology you may need help with. Working on training and professional development can take several directions.

Identify skill gaps

Start by recognizing your skill gaps by writing them down on paper. The more we leave them sitting back in the cloudy corners of our brains, the more the nagging thoughts of "I need to manage this" remain! So get them written out. Get the needs written on a whiteboard so everyone in the office can see them. Ask for a teammate or partner to help hold you accountable while you undergo the process.

Next, with the list of skill gaps written out, award yourself a skill rating. One through five? Or one through ten? Either way, take a few minutes with that mindset moment to give yourself two ratings for each skill gap: what level you're starting from and where you'd like to be.

Some key areas to strengthen business development and forecasting that benefit business owners are strategic planning, forecasting, merchandising, and reading data (key performance indicators, KPIs). But it's important you identify your unique skill gaps.

The fun part begins when we ask someone else to evaluate this list and these numbers. As entrepreneurs, we must employ our resources, so call a fellow business owner and see if they will review this with us. You might be surprised because that fellow business owner might have suggestions or tools ready on the call to share free information immediately to help you with your skill gaps!

Find the right training program

You can find so much training online. The digital education explosion post-COVID-19 has introduced a wealth of online resources, making training more accessible yet overwhelming.

Chapter 7

Whether it's a thorough analysis of technology systems, a seminar on strategic planning, or a hands-on workshop in data analysis, prioritization, leadership, or social media management, you have endless options available. Choose wisely, and I'll be happy to help! You might remember that my favorite number for evaluation is three. So, pick three training options and make a pro and con list for each.

For those tackling specific areas like target marketing or consumer psychology, consider tailored courses that offer both theoretical and practical knowledge. Remember, the most effective learning often occurs in interactive environments, so while online courses offer convenience, the hands-on guidance of in-person training is needed.

Beyond social media and marketing skills, it's easy today to find a billion companies ready to help us grow. Still, I will warn you: some online courses need to be more practical for this type of training. Consider taking a course at a local university instead and paying for a service on a long-term basis, in person, and with guided support available during the education period. Many of the courses I've seen available online are self-driven, and at least 50 percent of humans need human interaction to learn.

Balancing this training with your daily responsibilities requires careful planning and commitment. Consider implementing a structured schedule that prioritizes key areas of development. Focus on one topic at a time to ensure depth and retention of knowledge. This approach facilitates a thorough understanding and allows for the practical application of new skills in real-world scenarios.

Consider Outsourcing

In our entrepreneurial journeys, we often encounter a familiar roadblock: the need for more time to sell and innovate, coupled with a pressing need to expand client bases and improve contact lists. To combat this, combine the essentials of professional development with strategic outsourcing. Outsourcing fills an immediate gap in capabilities and serves as a strategic lever to enhance business operations. Before you begin, evaluate!

Identify areas of need

The first step is to analyze which aspects of the business would benefit most from seeking external expertise. Consider digital marketing needs, CRM, inside or outside sales, or specific technical tasks within your operations.

Select the right partners

The ideal outsourcing partners should be affordable, have a firm grasp of your industry, and share the same business goals as your company. Whether you work with a freelance consultant or opt for a specialized agency, their expertise must align perfectly with your specific needs. I will elaborate on this matter in a moment. Still, I cannot stress strongly enough the need for us to conduct a comprehensive investigation into our partnership relationships for outsourcing. A helpful analogy for understanding this process is to think of it as lending money to a friend. I refuse to do it. If someone requires financial assistance, I am more than willing to provide a gift without any anticipation of repayment to maintain the harmony of our relationship should any complications arise.

Evaluate and adapt

Regularly assess the effectiveness of outsourced services and adjust as needed. This responsiveness will help you stay aligned with changing business objectives and market conditions. I've made some financial mistakes in this department and am not afraid to admit it!

One of my contractor hires last year was a disaster. A $4,000 investment, which was "guaranteed" to build at least that in ROI, has only returned $500 to date. Thankfully, I could negotiate with the contractor and devise a plan without losing the relationship. To this day, she is still working for me to make up for the lack of ROI. I'll consider this a lucky outcome and a graceful partnership. Still, it's caused me to be more careful in my approach to subs and outsourcing and helped me read the fine print in contracts more carefully.

Implement outsourcing as a strategic tool

Embracing outsourcing can help you do more, deliver better service, and grow your business faster. This strategy lets you address skill gaps, handle costs efficiently, and prioritize high-return areas.

The bottom line is that outsourcing is not only about finding support—it's about smartly boosting our businesses to tackle challenges and seize opportunities. If we play our cards right and team up with the right partners, outsourcing can really take us to the next level and help us fight some serious competition.

Examples

Lighting design consultant: Rachel, an experienced lighting designer and owner of Illuminate Designs, needed help to justify her consultancy fees. She **outsourced her marketing and branding** to a creative agency, which repositioned her business as a premium service provider through a targeted branding strategy.  This strategic move helped Rachel communicate the value of her services more effectively, leading to increased client acquisition and project wins.

Custom door and hardware showroom: Sarah, the owner of Artisan Doors and More, found it challenging to manage customer relationships amid daily operations. With the help of a technology consultant, she invested in a CRM system customized for her business. This tool centralized cus-  tomer interactions, streamlined follow-ups, and integrated with her marketing platforms, enhancing customer service *and engagement*.

Mom-and-pop hardscape center: Mark and Lisa's small hardscape center, Greenscapes Depot, needed a cohesive online presence. They enlisted a digital advertising agency that developed a tailored brand strategy, created custom radio and television ads

to attract more local audiences, and engaged customers with local events. This approach significantly increased their market reach and customer engagement.

Flooring and paint retail showroom: Flooring and Paint Studio One faced revenue constraints that limited their ability to hire full-time outside sales staff. They opted to hire freelance professionals to help advertise during specific times of the year, which improved their marketing consistency and effectiveness without needing permanent staff.

Learn to Delegate

I recently collaborated with a group of women to plan a baby shower. During this event planning, I realized I am more accustomed to delegating tasks than many of my nonbusiness friends and associates. The request from the host for assistance to bring food and help with the games and planning launched eighty group text messages and drove me insane! I finally called the host and volunteered to help wherever she needed. I suggested it would be easier if she could assign individuals a "task" and create a sign-up sheet, like making the shopping registry! Allowing your business partner or staff to see the list of tasks required and select the one that fits their budget or time constraints would alleviate the pressure from the host while also allowing our community to contribute to a more significant cause. The host agreed and quickly went to find an online task monkey helper service. Realizing that this solution isn't evident to many prompted me to include this section in this chapter.

Consider learning to delegate and accepting the outcome as part of your training and development. Dale Carnegie, an industry leader in professional development, wrote, "Delegation isn't just about moving stuff off your plate. It's about developing others while efficiently achieving specific organizational outcomes. Delegation takes work on a leader's part to determine who is ready for specific assignments and who can take ownership while not taking control."[39]

Decide What's Best for You!

Take this very moment to commit to your professional development.

I understand your challenges because I've also experienced them. With over twenty-five years of experience in the industry, Rep Methods' dynamic seminars, workshops, personalized coaching, and boot camps aim to transform your business approach and boost your market success. Join us, and let's turn your potential into real-world performance. Discover how Alison's strategies through Rep Methods can help you excel in your business endeavors and make every sales opportunity count. Embrace this chance to refine your strategy and market with precision—your journey to top-tier sales effectiveness starts now.

---

[39] "Delegation," Dale Carnegie Course #258, [accessed Aug 2024] https://www.dalecarnegie.com/en/courses/258

CHAPTER 8
Embracing Technology, Rethinking Leverage

The exciting world of technology. We are living in an extraordinary time! The only way to stay on track incorporating technology into our strategy is to run to a search engine whenever we find a blip in our productivity. Having been both a salesperson and a small business owner, I am overwhelmed by the visibility required of my brand. If it weren't for technology, no one would know what I'm doing and connect with my brand.

Chapter 8

It's incredible to see how far our society has advanced and all the tools available. I hope to highlight practical tools and resources specifically designed for immediate implementation.

Innovation is happening rapidly, with new companies constantly developing innovative software applications. Testimonial videos are now all the rage, so display your work with clients in clips. In just this year, I've found several online programs to help with efficiency, saving me countless hours of video editing. Originally, a three-minute video took me a minimum of three hours to complete. As a marketing creative, I relied heavily on the correlation between the length of the video and the hours of edits required. Now, I have purchased an app called Munch[40] that creates clips for me from hour-long tutorials; it will even caption it! I have plug-and-play video apps like Microsoft Clip Champ[41], and if you recall the story I told you in Chapter 4, I use Deep Reel[42] within Canva[43] which generates an avatar to be the actor in my videos using a script. It's amazing how fast technology is changing marketing. But it's changing our sales pitch tactics too! I frequently use Gamma[44] to help me start slide deck presentations. If you haven't already used OpenAI software like ChatGPT, which can research anything for you, OpenAI also has a sales call software that will provide cold-calling services from a computer that sounds like a human. I must admit it's scary; however, just like the internet was scary, new technology will continue to refine, and the stars will shine on the highest performers. It's also something big for me to embrace some of

---

[40] App.getmunch.com
[41] App.clipchamp.com
[42] Beta.deepreel.com
[43] www.canva.com
[44] Gamma.app

this technology as much as I boast going back to old fashioned methods like simply picking up the phone.

This chapter will focus on the latest and greatest with a sincere reboot for those using CRM systems. Let's start by talking about what we are *not* doing with our data, for those of us who have systems in place and if you haven't invested in one, maybe you'll get some ideas for what you need.

What Are We Doing Wrong?

Data: clean, useable, amazing data. It's the essential ingredient we need to gain perspective. **Customer Relationship Management** (CRM) systems help us pull data in the following ways:

- what we sell
- how we sell
- who we sell to
- merchandising strategies
- inventory management
- cost analysis
- sales profit and loss
- project management
- follow-up
- customer relationship data
- sales timelines

And more. So, yes, most businesses can benefit from a system that can help you do all the above.

One of my clients in Texas vehemently proclaimed he wanted me to refrain from discussing CRM tactics during one of my sales training workshops, but managers and team leaders often miss crucial aspects of data usage, and they misinterpret how to empower their sales staff better by relaying and training how to use that data more effectively. In the last year, I came across two scenarios:

- A client needed a reorganization of customer data to assist in digging through the muck and confusion of selling and follow-up, entering quotes, cold calling, and beyond.
- A client had CRM but wasn't using its power effectively because they didn't "have enough time to pull reports or analyze data" and didn't "know where to get started using that data."

> **Pro Tip!** Feel free to make notes in the columns and take them back to your manager or owner and ask for help pulling data from an existing system.

You may be in one of those scenarios. Let's get you using data more effectively. systems have revolutionized how businesses manage their interactions with customers and prospects. Effective use of data systems can lead to enhanced customer satisfaction, increased sales, and improved operational efficiency.

Every interaction captured in a data management system translates into data points that can drive significant business decisions. However, entering data is just the first step; the crucial work begins with its analysis and application. Despite the power of these systems, they are often underutilized because of a lack of training or the overwhelming nature of data.

Imagine data as your strategic advisor. Businesses and salespeople often make sales direction, or marketing, decisions based on guesswork, kind of like the old adage "throwing spaghetti against the wall," or "putting the cart before the horse." While guesswork might occasionally work, we could be more efficient, right? Hone our skills and intuition, right? Instead, business owners need to anticipate customer needs, tailor those marketing efforts, and streamline operations by analyzing trends and patterns in data, ensuring that every decision is informed and strategic. We've done so much work already to strengthen our sales strategy, brand strategy, and marketing plans, let's take it a step further and understand how implementing one of these systems can help us tweak our strategies even more.

Benefits of a CRM system

Primarily, a CRM centralizes the data of every client, vendor, subcontractor, or affiliate business you or your team interacts with daily. For an account and sometimes an inventory powerhouse system, tons of options are available based on each business's primary functionality. For example, POS systems for restaurants and retailers centralize core inventory, sales data, and customer information so that this B2C business can, over time, develop trends, forecast sales, and shift their brand based on customer traffic. A company with this type of system is sure to succeed in a short amount of time.

Customers shift, loyalty shifts, and our brands must change with the market, or we will fail. By analyzing the trends and sales over periods, we know how to make inventory changes and tweak our target personas to shift and align with our primary customers. As for B2B wholesalers and vendors with accounts and clients, these can run into the hundreds, if not thousands, within one geographic region. The number of clients will help determine the required staff needed to keep customers happy and sales flowing. Account management, along with inventory management, are the primary data collectors for these businesses. Storing important shipping and billing data, tracking sales, and logging years of data have become priorities in applying the same principles of a B2B. We must use this data to guide our stocking priorities and shift brand strategy toward niche customers to maintain brand loyalty. As an account manager for many years, sometimes with hundreds of clients, it's only possible to remember some of their purchase history and preferences. These systems make our lives easy. We can take notes and log specific data, which anyone in the team can access to find quick and easy answers to build better relationships and sales.

These systems help us focus on market segmentation and personalization, which allows for personalized communication and marketing efforts, significantly enhancing customer engagement and loyalty. Personalization can include tailored email campaigns, customized product recommendations, and personalized customer service interactions.

They also provide data-driven decision-making, giving us valuable insights through data analytics and reporting tools. Businesses can track KPIs, analyze customer behavior, and measure the effectiveness of marketing campaigns. These insights help us make informed decisions, identify trends, and predict future customer needs.

CRMs were the first AI! Just kidding, but for outside salespeople, CRMs began helping us automate routine tasks. I have often missed having one as a small business. I loved it when my sales force helped me set up my calendar. I loved being able to set reminders for follow-up emails and scheduling appointments. I loved pulling a list of clients and staring at it! Yes, by simply having my "account list" in a paper format at my desk, I could routinely scroll through quietly with my ruler and identify names of people or businesses I missed on my last visit. Then I could carefully determine which clients might need a phone call or check-in.

Scrolling through the account list would prompt me to take notes on specific tasks I needed to follow up on, and a CRM system can automate this, saving time and allowing employees to focus on more strategic activities. For example, sales teams can automate the follow-up process for leads, ensuring potential customers are noticed and printing is optional.

Automations have saved my life since starting a business and website. Now as a small business, I use my web host software as a moderate CRM. It works the same way as the more prominent investment software. I use Wix, and I'm not promoting it for any other reason than the user interface, which acts as a CRM system for me as a small business. It automates emails and stores my customer data and sales history like a CRM.

CRM systems should be integrated with other business tools like email marketing platforms, accounting software, and e-commerce systems. Integration ensures seamless data flow between different systems, eliminating data silos and providing a unified view of customer interactions. Schedule a free demo with a company and ask all the right questions about your current systems for exact interface information. For example, check with your invoicing and financial system to see if they also have a CRM system.

Chapter 8

Why aren't we using the data?

A good data system starts with the human responsible for entering the data! Poor data entry quality will undermine the effectiveness of a system. Businesses must establish data governance practices to ensure data is accurate, complete, and current. I recommend data entry policies for all employees and yourself if you are an entrepreneur following guidelines and regular audits! If you require inside and outside sales staff to enter data, how often are you checking their/your data entry? Accountability is essential if we expect to utilize our investment.

How are you using the data? Why aren't you using the data?

Yes, I'm looking directly at you!

This is by far the most frustrating for a trainer or manager. Speaking as the salesperson who still regularly enters data into their internal system, it is very frustrating and saddening when I find out clients aren't training their staff to use the data provided to their advantage. They will spend all their spare time entering data into a system, yet they make decisions without consulting the data.

With correct information, we can quickly identify our top-performing customers, and we can begin to identify niche segments where we will be most successful in procuring new business.

Other Technologies

Investing in apps and proper data management can make or break your time management. As I stated in the opening of this chapter, there are tons of new technology programs helping me with time management and data processing. Investing in these technology-based assets can help us speed up how we process all the historical sales data, make us faster and help build our sales intuition. Remember, data is the tool we need to make decisions properly. In this section I'll outline some technology wins that are helping me in my entrepreneurial journey. It's also a good idea to include a note about how quickly this chapter will age out. Technology is moving so quickly; I hate to think that in five years some of these programs or services might be obsolete. I try to keep up with the times, and for now, I'm feeling at the forefront of my generation (elder millennials) in embracing what AI is doing to change our lives and I just hope I can keep up and AI is helping me stay functional and move faster with my data.

Calendar booking/appointment booking services

These literally save me time daily, but I've seen people employ them poorly, so let's take a look at the technology I've found and find the ones that work for you.

With the evolution of phone calendars syncing with Outlook, Gmail, Yahoo, and all the other email services, using technology to help you book appointments and automate keeping up with appointments is simple. Most people with a bit of experience scheduling meetings have the general concept of setting up the calendar appointment in their email accounts and carefully crafting every detail, such as timing, time zone, video conferencing option, and meeting details. I used to spend at least twenty minutes just setting up an appointment on my calendar until I employed Calendly[45] and CalendarBridge[46] daily! I manage six personal and business email accounts for companies and my email account for the brands I represent. It's a lot! CalendarBridge helps me link all the emails back to a master account to ensure every single appointment will be copied to the master calendar system.

Bulk email and marketing helpers

I mentioned Constant Contact[47] regarding their bulk text statistics in the last chapter. This is just one of the many companies available to help us filter through the thinking required for mass marketing strategies. Some other companies have notably improved their services over the years: Gmail now has GMass,[48] where for small fees, Gmail users can send spam protective mass emails, automate follow-up, schedule out marketing plans, analyze the behavior of their audiences, and have assistance building their email list. GMass can perform tests, check links, and verify emails before hitting send! Amazing stuff!

Texting

Forbes published an article in August 2024 ranking these companies as the best bulk texting software available: ClickSend, Trumpia, Textedly, Clickatell, SendPulse, TextMarks, and BulkSMS.[49]

---

[45] Calendly: https://calendly.com/app/login.
[46] CalendarBridge: https://app.calendarbridge.com/login.
[47] Constant Contact: https://www.constantcontact.com/.
[48] GMass owned by Google and Gmail: https://www.gmass.co/
[49] "The Best Mass Texting Services of 2024," *Forbes Advisor*, accessed August 19, 2024, https://www.forbes.com/advisor/business/software/best-mass-texting-services/.

I don't use this type of service, as it's not right for my business, so I can't verify or support these remarks. However, it will be something I employ in the near future as my audience grows and I have more online events needing reminders.

As a small business owner, using these add-on services with other marketing service agencies like Constant Contact would be more suitable for me as a "one-stop shop" to avoid having a hundred subscriptions with varying companies.

It's a perfect opportunity to talk about AI because now, with OpenAI, even technology can call and text for us to generate leads.

Video creative software for social media clips

Are you a coach? Do you often hold sessions online? Ever wonder what you could do with all that video footage from Zoom recording? Get yourself a program like Munch.[50] When uploading any recording, no matter the length, Munch spits out clips so you can customize the look for the captions, and bam, you have social-ready content on a dime. It can even post for you if you don't already use a service for social scheduling.

Social scheduling

You need to follow a strategy if you aren't using social scheduling within your marketing plan. Companies like Later,[51] Loomly,[52] Mailchimp,[53] Sprout Social,[54] Buffer,[55]

---

[50] Munch: https://app.getmunch.com/
[51] Later: https://later.com/
[52] Loomly: https://www.loomly.com/
[53] Mailchimp: https://mailchimp.com/
[54] Sprout Social: https://sproutsocial.com/
[55] Buffer: https://buffer.com/

Hootsuite,[56] Zoho[57], and more help you do this. I've used all of these services over the years and found them all to be helpful. I have needed to upgrade and change services when managing multiple businesses' social feeds. Look at the offerings for each and make sure they already work with the software you use. They will allow you to set creative time each week and schedule your social media months in advance if necessary. Some also offer more live tracking analytics toward the ever-changing algorithms so you don't have to keep up with the trends.

AI

Rethink the way you once viewed AI. What if AI is about something other than robots doing all the work? What if they could help us refine our thinking in a way we can't see? I'm quickly becoming an expert at using this technology in my day to day to help me buy back time. As a Xennial, I grew up reading books and playing outside. Still, as the Netflix generation has progressed, my streaming of National Geographic or the remake of a literary marvel is typically taken visually, not tucked away in a muted nook with a book. Plus, my ADD-style brain can't sit still longer than an hour and a half. Using AI has transformed not only my writing skills but also my marketing abilities and conception of presentations.

AI helps me think outside the box, my box, i.e., my limited brain! I'm not so egocentric to think I know everything or that I have all the answers, or that my way is the only way. AI has allowed for exploratory missions down paths beyond my conception. Essentially, it's like having a virtual assistant who

---

[56] Hootsuite: https://www.hootsuite.com/
[57] Zoho: https://www.zoho.com/

can help me refine what my brain wants to say but my mouth can't process, or my writing can't expel. To the critics of the world who say, "That's cheating," it's not. I'm harnessing the brainpower of millions of thinkers to help me outline what I really wanted to say. I'm starting to view AI as my new dictionary. When I was a kid, my dad would make me jump up from the kitchen table and run for the dictionary whenever I couldn't spell a word or inevitably asked, "What does that mean?" at the dinner table. Think about the time it takes to run over to the shelf, pull down that big book, and flip through its pages to find this infamous new "palabra" I would soon add to my nine-year-old vocabulary. I would read and process the definition, and then move on about my day. Soon instead of a dictionary, it became Google. Now AI is simply the new Google. Instead of waiting for Google, Bing, Yahoo, Apple, or whatever to spit out the correlated websites and decide what is relevant, AI processes that data for you in milliseconds. Instead of fumbling through a million pages of data pulled together in the search engine, the same concept is happening right before your eyes, and typically, once learning your "style," it's formulated in a manner that meets your expectations and cuts time into nothing.

Imagine being able to harness AI for sales, transforming your business and its voice, and capitalizing all this time we can get back to doing research. Imagine AI might even be heading (quickly) to the ability to know us so well it can answer questions about us, not just generalizations or typical demographics, but know and understand what we will choose, what we want, and what we don't even know we want as consumers. What if your company can harness this power to make the selection process easier for all these topics we have discussed in this book thus far: **marketing, merchandising, relationship building, retention strategies, follow-up,** and beyond?

While attending a conference in San Diego, I was introduced to a remarkable product, person, and company using AI to transform the general contractor's position in the construction industry. Sarah Buchner, Founder and CEO of Trunk Tools, told her story of innovation in our industry and how her company is transforming the research perspective and problem-solving skills surrounding the primary target market of this conference, which were large general contractor firms from California and beyond. Trunk Tools harnesses the power of AI to spit out solutions for contractors to resolve based upon reading the details included in millions of pages of drawings and specifications for billion-dollar projects. For example, let's say they were in the execution process and discovered the details for a receptacle missing from the blueprints. Typically, it would take many hours for the project managers and teams to go back through the designs/drawings/blueprints to find the correct item, replace it, and then submit it for approval. Instead, the AI program, Trunk Tools, cuts through the fat, time-wasting process of hunting, gathering, and approval by simply searching *within* the existing documents to find the missing information and, within seconds, implement the remedy.[58]

AI-powered analytics tools can analyze construction project data, such as project timelines, material requirements, and

---

[58] Buchner, Sarah. "Transforming the Construction Industry with AI: The Story of Trunk Tools." Presentation at Groundbreaking Women in Construction, San Diego, CA, May 17, 2024.

budget constraints, to provide insights and recommendations for optimizing construction processes and enhancing project efficiency.

AI-driven virtual assistants can assist construction professionals with project planning, scheduling, and resource allocation, streamlining project management tasks and improving overall productivity, scheduling, and task list creation! I haven't joined the virtual assistant movement, but it is an interesting concept, especially for solopreneur businesses that always need an extra set of hands. That doesn't mean you shouldn't consider these initiatives for yourself.

As I mentioned in the section opener, cold-calling AI bots are the new rage. These aren't just tools; they're revolutionizing the lead-generation process for businesses like mine. Here's how they work: the AI meticulously tracks potential customers who are already a fit for our products and within our target market. It doesn't stop there. The bot identifies the decision-maker, makes the initial call, and skillfully navigates through the lead capture process. AI cold-calling services spare the user from the most daunting part of sales—the dreaded cold call. No more dialing number after number, battling to get a live lead on the line, and coaxing out details to move them from mere inquiry to readiness to purchase. Hiring out in this manner looks to be a monumental relief for a small business owner like me, who simply doesn't have the time to chase down call lists. These bots help push our consumer or B2B sales efforts into reality more efficiently.

Let me share a real-life example of how predictive analytics dramatically improved our sales outcomes. Our sales team was struggling with a plateau in closure rates despite an increase in lead generation. We decided to implement an AI-driven predictive analytics tool to gain deeper insights into our sales process and customer preferences.

The AI analyzed patterns in our historical sales data and identified key factors most indicative of a successful close. Armed with this information, our sales team refined their pitches, focusing on the elements that were likely to resonate with potential customers. They tailored their approaches based on each lead's predicted preferences and readiness. The results were nothing short of remarkable. Within just a few months of using these insights to guide our pitches, we saw a 30 percent increase in closure rates. The AI not only helped us understand our customers better but also taught us how to adjust our strategies dynamically to meet market demands.

See, AI in sales isn't just about automation; it's about enhancing human capabilities and making every customer interaction more strategic and effective. By incorporating AI tools like lead scoring and predictive analytics, businesses can not only increase efficiency but also achieve a level of insight and precision that was previously unattainable. In the fast-paced world of sales, staying ahead means staying informed, and AI is the key to unlocking that potential.

Otter.ai[59]:

This AI program can make note-taking and transcribing all those video calls and podcasts a breeze! This fantastic addition to your repetition will allow you to go back to the conversation when you are ready, freeing up those precious moments post-

---

[59] Otter.ai: https://otter.ai/

meeting or call and eliminating us from scrambling to take notes during a conversation.

Virtual reality (VR) and augmented reality (AR)

VR and AR technology can revolutionize the construction industry by allowing stakeholders to visualize building designs and construction plans in immersive 3D environments.

Virtual walk-throughs and AR overlays enable architects, engineers, and clients to explore construction projects, identify potential issues, and make informed decisions before construction begins.

In the construction industry, I've seen this work for small businesses. A friend of mine owns a granite fabrication shop up in Ashland, VA. This Brazilian family has always been at the forefront of technology and implementing innovative selling strategies. Still, as one of their sons came of age and began to take over the business for his dad, the innovation took an entirely new level. Chris worked with a third-party enterprising software company to implement three or four specific room layouts and created a space to add materials from his warehouse. He made a space for customers to view natural vs. engineered stone in their kitchen while adding flooring and tile. This type of technology is still coming around; we cannot yet add every color, swatch, tile, stone, or surface into such a database. However, this type of enterprise gave small businesses an edge. It gave them something unique to advertise and something to get customers in their doors to try it out for themselves. This one innovation increased their lead opportunities tenfold. And imagine the outcome of using the devices at local and regional home shows. The ability to give that showroom experience and connect with their potential client, regardless of its accuracy, created value and a niche experience tailored toward their target customer. I'll personally be waiting for the company that launches this type of technology with the ability to upload live inventory into the software for a more accurate and probable visualization. When that comes, sign me up for the sales team. I'm in!

Innovative equipment and IoT devices

Innovative construction equipment embedded with sensors and IoT devices can monitor performance, track usage patterns, and predict maintenance needs, reducing downtime and optimizing equipment utilization. Examples include **smart cranes** equipped with sensors to monitor load weight and distribution or **IoT-enabled bulldozers** that track operational efficiency and predict maintenance needs. **Smart concrete** embedded with sensors can detect stress levels, temperature, and humidity, helping to monitor a structure's health in real time.

IoT-enabled construction materials, such as intelligent concrete and structural sensors, can provide real-time data on material strength, integrity, and environmental conditions, ensuring quality control and compliance with project specifications.

These technologies are related to how insurance companies and fleet services monitor vehicles. Companies now have the ability to track vehicle performance, predict maintenance, and monitor employee behavior. Does anyone have that progressive device boasted to promote safe driving and reduce insurance rates? I do!

This concept can also be applied to showroom products. For instance, IoT devices could be embedded in showroom areas to monitor salesperson and customer interactions, track wear and tear, and even gather data on environmental conditions like temperature and humidity that I think will affect the products on display.

Depending on the product or service you offer, you can add smart technology that can enhance product management and customer experience by ensuring optimal product maintenance and data-driven decisions about product placement and display.

Predictive analytics and demand forecasting

Predictive analytics tools can analyze market trends, demand for specific materials, and regional economic factors to forecast demand and inform procurement decisions.

By leveraging predictive analytics, suppliers and distributors can optimize inventory levels, anticipate material shortages, and ensure timely delivery of construction materials to meet project deadlines.

A variety of companies and simple apps enable even small businesses to enhance project efficiency, improve decision-making, and deliver exceptional results in today's results driven and logistically challenged market. For many of us, those exist within those pesky CRM systems I keep discussing! If this is something you need, I suggest consulting with a few of the small business-based CRM companies mentioned earlier to ensure their analytics and any reporting are easy for you to access and interpret.

For example, many of my clients use an inventory management control system called Stone Profits. The system is designed not only for managing inventory but also for keeping customer data, quoting and estimations, sales orders, invoicing and account management, but I'm always amazed at how many employees don't know how to use the data reporting to help them with sales. Analytic reports are our keys to forecasting and managing inventory, tracking and creating future sales, keeping current sales ongoing, and tracking sales we might be about to lose.

Some companies now offer big and colorful visual dashboards aiding us in reviewing key performance indicators (KPIs) daily, but be sure to check if this is something available within your price range when investing in a software plan.

Finally, just as we discussed in the last chapter, invest in training or hire an analytical specialist. Regardless of visual dashboards with magic colorful callouts to our KPIs, make sure you are knowledgeable on how to use them!

Identifying costs

In brief, technology, AI, and VR are not reserved solely for large corporations. They hold the potential to be effective tools for small businesses to prosper in today's competitive retail sector. By harnessing the power of these tools, we can fine-tune our strategies, create captivating shopping experiences, and ultimately, drive sales and foster business growth.

When venturing into new technology investments, a meticulous cost-benefit analysis is paramount for ensuring that the financial decisions bolster the business's strategic goals. This systematic approach not only forecasts the potential returns but also aligns the investment with the organization's operational needs and long-term objectives.

Initial investment. This includes the outright purchase price and any expenses related to installation and integration into existing systems. It's crucial to account for all upfront costs to gauge the actual starting point of the investment.

Operational cost. Beyond the initial expenditure, fees and renewals have to be considered, especially if revenue is modest in the first year or so. These recurring expenses might include licensing fees, routine maintenance, and staff training to use the new technology adeptly. These factors contribute significantly to the overall financial commitment and impact the viability of the investment.

Calculate ROI.

ROI = Total Benefits − Total Costs − Total costs X 100

Taking the time to finalize ROI and analyzing the payback period—the time it takes for the benefits to repay the costs—will give you confidence in the investment.

Customer satisfaction. Enhanced technological capabilities often lead to improved customer experiences. This enhancement can significantly boost customer satisfaction and loyalty, leading to repeat business and referrals that may not be immediately apparent in initial ROI calculations.

Consider brand reputation. Investing in the latest technology can strengthen a company's position in the market. It sends a message of innovation and responsiveness to evolving market needs, enhancing brand perception and leading to increased market share.

Chapter 8

Conclusion

Adopting new technologies is essential for businesses seeking to enhance efficiency and stay competitive. However, the **process often introduces challenges** that can hinder successful adoption.

One of the most common **barriers** to technology adoption is **resistance** within the organization. People are often comfortable with existing processes and may view new technologies as disruptive or threatening. To mitigate resistance, announce the benefits of the new technology before getting started with staff. Providing detailed explanations of how technology will improve specific aspects of workflow, increasing job efficiency, or providing other personal benefits can help change perceptions and garner support.

Don't forget to carve out time for **training**. Providing comprehensive and accessible training is essential. You need to ensure that all users have the resources and support they need to become proficient with the new technology. Training should be tailored to different learning styles and competencies to maximize effectiveness and comfort with the technology.

Using innovative tools helps streamline operations and gain insights into customers and market trends. We should prioritize improving the people behind the machines, despite the greatness of technology. Let's go back to the root cause of our operational troubles: we're **human**.

SECTION 3

Mastering Target the Human Element

A Psychological and Operational Aspect of Sales

Humans create life. Literally, at our most basic level, we bring life to the table. We also keep the world interesting, don't we? With our art, music, food and of course, technology! Yes, we've needed humans to advance technology too! With the progress of AI, do you think there is a risk people will no longer need to rely on their cognitive abilities and instincts? Will the Covid-19 generation, who stand to come of age in 2037, feel the need to prioritize emotional intelligence in their professional lives? Will they need to find empathy in sales? Will body language still matter in thirty years? I hope so.

While our reliance on phones and computers is undeniable, section three *of Beyond Order Makers* highlights the importance of the human element in selling, examining the **human psychological and operational aspects of sales** that cannot be replaced.

We're going to cover some of the most requested topics from my sales training workshops and seminars as well as a brand new, inventive approach to **manifesting sales**, increasing our profitability & forming an infallible pipeline, or as I like to call it, *the snowball*.

Brace yourself for a captivating trip down memory lane as we discuss fresh insights on **buyer psychology** and dive into the ever-fascinating land of **emotional intelligence**. In addition, I aim to shed light on how we can rescue ourselves from self-sabotaging behaviors with a conversation on **work-life balance.** Meanwhile don't miss the all-important chapter on the **operational improvements** you will transform, highlighting the crucial role that **organization and time management** play in enhancing our productivity. So get transformation ready my young phoenix.

CHAPTER 9
The Human Element
Emotional Intelligence and Selling

At the heart of every successful close is a genuine human connection that evolved over time. Genuine connections start forming inside the human psyche from the onset of any interaction human or digital.

In this chapter, I want to show you how sales professionals can move beyond surface-level transactions and engage customers on a deeper, more meaningful level.

Chapter 9

Remember that finessing a sale from lead to close is about being proactive and building an infallible intuition to move things forward. Thinking forward, moving forward. Before we even reach the sales pitch, the process of closing sales is already in motion, pushing the client towards a positive conclusion. If we want to excel in sales, we must familiarize ourselves with how the human body and psyche operate. That's Emotional Intelligence (EI).

Central to this approach is the concept of limbic resonance, which highlights the power of emotional connection in human interactions. When applied to sales, it enables you to capture your customer's undivided attention, creating a moment where they feel truly heard and understood. This connection not only builds trust but also lays the foundation for loyalty and long-term relationships.

It's important to remember that it's our humanness—our unique ability to read emotions, interpret subtle cues, and build intuitive understanding—that makes these connections possible. No technology can replicate this intuitive sense of empathy or anticipate the complexities of human emotions in real-time. This chapter focuses on embracing and enhancing that human element, allowing you to navigate the nuances of human interaction with confidence and authenticity.

In this chapter we'll dive into the following principles of using EI during the sales process.

- **Active Listening:** The foundation of any successful sales conversation, where we focus not only on hearing but understanding what the client truly needs, even when they aren't explicitly stating it.

- **Establishing Expertise:** Building trust by confidently showcasing your knowledge and experience, while remaining relatable and authentic.
- **Empathy:** Stepping into the client's shoes to genuinely understand their feelings, concerns, and motivations, and responding with care and sincerity.
- **Managing Reactivity:** Staying composed and adaptable in any sales situation, especially when faced with objections or challenging emotions.
- **Body Language:** Understanding and responding to nonverbal cues, which often communicate more than words alone and allow for deeper connections.
- **Creating Customized Experiences:** Tailoring every interaction to the individual client, showing them that their needs and preferences are valued and understood.

This human-centric approach enables you to cultivate relationships that go beyond immediate sale, paving the way for long-term success and client loyalty. Let's start with one of the fan favorites: *limbic resonance*.

Limbic Resonance

Limbic resonance uses emotional intelligence to transform the effectiveness of our sales process. A delicate dance between all of the aforementioned actions, we create genuine connections by actively listening to clients, showing expertise, exhibiting empathy, leveraging emotional intelligence, discerning nonverbal cues, managing emotional reactions, and prioritizing personalized sales strategies. Forming connections enhances the sales process and contributes to long-term client relationships and loyalty.

By focusing on the human element in each of these components, we elevate our approach from **transactional to transformative, from reactive to proactive**, ultimately leading to more tremendous success in closing deals. In my first book, I delved into the transformative power of limbic resonance as detailed in Daniel Goleman, Richard E. Boyatzis, and Annie McKee's work, *Primal Leadership*.[60] This concept is a tool in emotional intelligence and a catalyst that can turn customer interaction into a profound connection. This is when all external distractions fade away, and the customer's undivided attention is captured, solidifying their commitment to the sales process.

As I often convey, success isn't just about pushing products; it's about forming genuine connections with clients. By understanding and implementing these basic elements, sales professionals can navigate the intricate dynamics of human interaction, ultimately paving the way for successful deal closures. This understanding empowers you to create meaningful connections that go beyond the transaction.

Not Actively Listening

Begin all sales conversations with as many questions as possible. The budget should be the last question because, typically, there will be one or two limiting technical or aesthetic factors that will narrow down the field of options for us! It's up to us to actively listen to the customers' needs and wants even when they aren't "telling" us directly about those important points, as I did with Jared.

---

[60] Daniel Goleman, Richard E. Boyatzis, and Annie McKee, *Primal Leadership: Realizing the Power of Emotional Intelligence* (Boston: Harvard Business School Press, 2002).

Over the years, I've watched salespeople attempting to sell by using the typical product data sheets that come from a marketing team. *This mini product knowledge session becomes their sales pitch*, throwing facts around and praying the client buys what they are selling based on bullet points from a flyer.

Over the winter, a client in Chicago asked if I could change this scenario for his sales team. The sales team was tasked with improving their selling techniques for a privately labeled product, which is usually more affordable compared to the brand name products they carry. In this case, the customer is seeking a compelling reason from the salesperson to opt for a private label product instead of well-known brands. While the motivation is typically price driven, there is sometimes a fear associated with downgrading to private-label products. This team was struggling to switch customers, and the managers struggled to build confidence in the sales team. It was my job to teach the importance of **active listening** during the conversation if the salespeople want to gather the *right* information building selling power. If salespeople probe more, we become in tune to the customers ask, we will *hear* the information required to build confidence in the private label brand and use that information to our selling advantage.

Active listening starts with asking questions. If our sales approach uses data and mostly jargon associated with the product, we will lose customers' attention and confuse them. Let me tell another personal story to convey a few right and wrong examples of the *limbic resonant & active listening dance*.

Chapter 9

Case Study: An In-home sales loss

Over the summer, I reached out to a friend from one of my industry groups, the Vice President of a local HVAC company, to get quotes for a new system. He decided to send one of his younger salespeople, Jared, to handle the consultation. Little did I know at the time, but my friend intentionally sent this greenhorn to see how he would handle the selling pro.

Jared introduced himself, and I explained my connection to one of his senior colleagues. Without much conversation, he immediately headed outside to inspect the outdoor unit, skipping over an initial sit-down or any preliminary questions. His sales pitch began with calculating the sizes needed for retrofitting or replacing the system. It seemed that Jared assumed my primary concern was finding the cheapest option, likely based on previous discussions with his boss, where I had inquired about discounted or sample stock opportunities.

From the outset, Jared framed his presentation with a "time-sensitive" pitch. He highlighted an upcoming regulation change at the end of 2024 that would increase prices due to new coolant standards and equipment overhauls. He effectively created urgency by warning me of these impending changes and asked if I was planning to make a purchase soon—tapping into the "fear factor" we will discuss in the next chapter as a technique to gauge client readiness.

However, I knew my interior closet height was a critical detail that would significantly narrow down the available options, so I guided Jared to the interior unit's return closet. We were spending too much time outside, discussing sizes without addressing other relevant factors. I then mentioned my concern with noise, given the small outdoor space and loud air vents in the townhome. Despite these hints, Jared didn't ask to run the existing unit or inquire about my specific preferences. Instead, I had to provide all the necessary details about noise levels and the outdoor unit's size requirements myself.

Eventually, after he measured the ceiling height, the available options became clearer. But even with these details, it was evident that Jared wasn't guiding the process. Instead, I had to direct him to three viable options based on my own knowledge and preferences. This highlighted a key issue: if I hadn't been an informed customer, or if my unit had completely failed and I was in a panic, the conversation would have been very different.

Jared's approach might have secured a sale, but it wouldn't have guaranteed my satisfaction. He didn't take the time to ask meaningful questions or actively listen to my concerns, leading him to miss key elements of what I needed. His confidence in promoting the first option as the superior choice wasn't enough to build trust. If he had been more attentive to relevant details like noise levels and space constraints, we could have narrowed it down to one or two strong possibilities, making the decision easier and more satisfactory.

In the end, Jared left without closing the deal because I didn't have confidence in the recommendations. I wasn't convinced that his company had the right equipment for my specific needs. If I didn't have prior knowledge, I might have chosen the least expensive option due to budget constraints, only to regret it later due to noise issues. For the next decade, I could have been stuck with a system that didn't meet my standards, simply because the salesperson didn't listen.

Active listening is fundamental to a successful sale. Jared's price-centric approach risked turning me into an unhappy customer prone to periodic complaints about noise or other issues. If you work in home improvement of any kind, we've all had *the problem customer* and if you are reading this and thinking of one, ask yourself if during the sales process active listening and a different product would have prevented the dissatisfaction. I believe the real job of a salesperson is to respond to customer-driven requirements and use emotional intelligence to provide a fulfilling solution and above all increases the likelihood for success post sale as well.

Establishing expertise

The next step is to establish expertise, increasing the likelihood of closing sales. In *The Art of Selling*, I asked my readers to dig deep and find their expertise. We all have one or more, and typically, it's a matter of confidence and sometimes takes a bit of encouragement from a senior manager, coach, or mentor to dig out the expertise within all of us. Recently, I volunteered again to aid with an industry mentorship program. During this process, we take candidates who have requested to be either mentees or mentors and perform interviews to decipher the best fit within our pool of candidates. I am amazed at the women who applied to be mentees and held positions like VP, senior director, owner, or president. By now, I fully support being humble and recognizing that we can all learn from someone else, but it's essential to know your worth and use that value to your advantage in the sales world. Becoming an expert in something takes work and humility. The human element in sales requires us to be that expert during a sales transaction. It's why companies don't send green new hires out into the field with little or no training. (If they do, it's not an excellent company for which to work/sell.)

Exhibiting our expertise and building rapport with a client lays the foundation for trust and confidence in decision making during sales. Even the greenest employees can dig deep to find a personal experience relatable to a customer. Finding that relatable moment is a big part of limbic resonance. You may recall my references to "chameleoning." Fostering communication by identifying with and becoming closer to the client's level will help the customer transform to respect our opinion. **Relatability** breeds **influence.** We can promote our **influence** by creating meaningful dialogue and a genuine interest in listening to the story or sequence started by our client.

Empathy

While establishing your expertise and engaging in the PK, you need to interpret the thoughts and needs of the consumer so you can have empathy. This means feeling out the customer's needs and analyzing the body language to share their feelings and perspectives. By putting ourselves into the client's shoes, we can anticipate clients' needs, craft responses, address concerns, and offer tailored solutions, a by-product of our expertise. Demonstrating empathy builds rapport and cultivates trust, which is essential for fostering long-term client relationships and driving repeat business.

We must leverage emotional intelligence through empathy, understanding, and managing one's emotions and those of others. Sales professionals with high emotional intelligence can adapt their approach to various client personalities, effectively navigate objections, and diffuse tense situations. We

Chapter 9

must consider the reactions, facial cues, body language, and tone of voice our client conveys. Ironically, this is where AI will fail us in the future. Will the computer be able to decipher these clues? (More about this in the chapter on technology and harnessing its power for sales.)

For now, this is the human element in selling: reading these critical sales indicators and listening with our eyes! We must watch and gauge a client's reaction to determine if we need to put another player at bat or switch gears to a more palatable subject. Determine if we will close today or if the client is wasting time, and we should plan to fold up the conversation quickly to maximize our time efficiency. Paying attention to what a client isn't saying can enable us to establish kinship more effectively, address concerns proactively, and guide the conversation toward a successful outcome.

Body Language

Let's examine a few positive and negative body language cues for closer inspection and more profound practice daily. If you recall a few experiences in conversations with clients lately, take a few minutes to play the tape back in your head, and you will recognize how body language played a role in the conversation.

Amy Cuddy has an excellent TED Talk with over seventy-one million views. In her discussion, she compares the **body language** of alphas vs introverts and gender body language.[61] I

---

[61] Cuddy, Amy. "Your Body Language May Shape Who You Are." Filmed June 2012. TED video, 21:02.
https://www.ted.com/talks/amy_cuddy_your_body_language_may_shape_who_you_are/transcript?language=en&subtitle=en.

learned that females are much more likely to exhibit powerful body language than their male counterparts.

Speaking of influential body language, women are now becoming the primary decision-makers for major purchases in their homes. Women are also the best at communicating with body language, as Cuddy describes.

According to Forbes Magazine, in 2024, purchases influenced by women were 85 percent.[62]

According to bankrate.com, in 2023, women make up 91 percent of new home purchases. So, if more than 80 percent of purchases and purchase influence are driven by women[63] and those women are the best at communicating with body language, it's time we start studying these concepts ASAP.

Let's talk about some specific body language to keep an eye out for when working on a sale or building relationships.

Open Arms vs. Crossed Arms

- Poor outcome: scowled face and crossed arms, huffy and puffy attitude, general impatience that you are in their presence either online or virtual.
- Change it: Ask if there is anything you can do to make them more comfortable.
- Ask if they are OK, if you're catching them at a bad time, or if they need to reschedule.

---

[62] Forbes. "Who Runs the World? Women Control 85 Percent of Significant Purchases." Last modified March 7, 2024. https://www.forbes.com/sites/digital-assets/2024/03/07/who-runs-the-world-women-control-85-percent/.
[63] Bankrate. "The Purchasing Power of Women: Statistics and Facts." Accessed June 2024. https://www.bankrate.com/loans/personal-loans/purchasing-power-of-women-statistics/#purchasing.

- ☺ Worst case, literally be up front about how their body language is making you feel and ask if something about this conversation needs to change. How can I make you happy, or what have I done to upset you?

- ☺ Addressing any "elephants" in the room and clearing the air will immediately result in significant body stance change.

- ☺ Hug it out. Is this a client who you feel is close enough personally that you would be comfortable offering them a hug? Do it—watch what happens!

Fidgeting

- ☹ Poor outcome: clasping and wringing hands, bouncing knees or feet, tapping fingers.

- 😕 Change it: Aim to get the head nod! Try to repeat some important affirmational facts that will appeal to this client's physiological needs. What do you know 100 percent is attractive and a win for them—aim to reinforce the positive.

- ☺ Offer the client some water or to move into a different room, as there is something about the space you are in that is making them uncomfortable.

- ☺ Ask if there is anything you can do to make them feel more at home.

Moving around vs. leaning in

- ☹ Poor outcome: If the client won't stop bouncing around the room or is focused on the computer screen adjacent to the one you are on, they aren't paying attention and aren't engaged, nor are they ready to close.

- 🤔 Change it: Ask if there is somewhere we can go sit down.
- 🙂 Ask if this is a bad time and you might need to wait a few minutes or reschedule.
- 🙂 Ask for their attention, explain why you need their full attention to be sure you are all on the same page, and throw in facts about their esteem needs that are waiting on this resolution.

Eye contact

- 😕 Poor outcome: If the person is checking behind you, looking away from the quote, paper, product, or sales item in question while you are talking, they are not going to buy from you and are not engaged in a transactional mindset.
- 🤔 Change it: Call their attention to the matter at hand directly, softly and kindly. Ask if this is a bad time and if they need to reschedule for a better moment.
- 🙂 Ask if you need to wait a few minutes while they finish their task at hand or softly exclaim, "I'll wait while you go handle that."

Chapter 9

 Rep Methods

BODY LANGUAGE COMPARISON

POSITIVE	NEGATIVE
 Open Arms / Stance	 Crossed Arms
 Leaning into the conversation	 Moving towards the door, or a different product
 Direct eye contact	 Looking down at the ground
 Head Nods	 Fidgeting

Manage our Reactivity

Effective salespeople recognize the impact of emotions on decision-making and employ strategies to manage their emotional reactions and those of their clients. By staying calm, composed, and empathetic, even in challenging situations, sales professionals can maintain control of the conversation and steer it toward a positive resolution.

I don't have the sales "poker face." I was not born with the ability to lie to anyone in person. Trust me, it stinks. For example, when a friend asks if I like her new jeans, I may think they aren't flattering, but I can't say things so bluntly! Sometimes, I wish I could lie through my teeth. Unfortunately, customers can see my reactions and emotions written all over my eyes, mouth, and head movements. Maintaining my belief in honesty being the best policy, I've had to tweak my sales "reactivity" around my limitations to hide my reactions. I must use my non-poker face to my advantage. Another powerful mechanism in controlling our reactivity is how we respond when we are told no or face rejection in sales. Often, inexperienced salespeople take the no and walk away, while experienced salespeople try to find out more reasons why the offer was rejected and attempt to reframe the conversation into a yes. One of the best ways to do this is by asking if we can review the winning bid or if the client would be willing to share what has made them choose the other consultant or agent. Using active listening and inquiry for details is the best power we have in changing the outcome or meeting the expectations at another time.

Chapter 9

Creating Customized Experiences

Above all, we must customize and cater each experience to the individual client.

Gone are the days of repeating sales pitches! I ask my students to craft a primary sales pitch and then begin to tweak the primary to all the various clientele who might walk in the door. I write and speak a lot about chameleoning, ironically, a trait I'm supposed to want to give up according to my twelve-step programs.

Because of this request by my recovery work, I have clung to learning more about this topic than an average Joe who couldn't care less if they fit in or not. I'd like you to consider chameleoning a chance to identify instead of considering it a fake persona. Chameleoning is an opportunity to customize my body language and communication from the moment a client walks in the door or appears on my screen.

If the customer is taking their precious time to work with us, visit our store, and execute our appointment request, what can we do to plan and make the experience go beyond their expectations? How can we accommodate and extend warmth and courtesy and prepare the best sell points that fit the client? Remember Jared? If he had taken five minutes to sit with me first, asking me what I wanted in an HVAC, the entire in-home sale would have gone in a different direction.

Action: First, find out what needs we must meet, fill in the blanks with the product options, and leave the rest out of the picture.

Remember the rule of three.

Remember, we can always replace a choice with something that suits the client better, but we limit their options and maximize our sales presentation.

As business owners and salespeople, we must be poised and prepared in all the above situations of our consumers' mindsets. For example, working with a retailer in Texas, I highlighted to my trainee the likelihood of a positive outcome when she was prepared for an appointment versus a walk-in consumer.

The more prepared we are before a sale or presentation, the more likely we are to close a deal. To familiarize you with the process, let's look at the stages and actions.

Preparation stage

In a perfect world, we would always have appointments, never spontaneous walk-in traffic or phone calls, and we could be prepared for every meeting. It's not a perfect world! But if we act as salespeople, we can do our best to uncover as much information as possible and be prepared (or spontaneous) when necessary, which increases the likelihood of closing a sale. According to the National Association of Sales Professionals, "Preparation is a difference maker. It separates the top sales teams from the inconsistent ones. Learn as much as possible about your potential client's operations and industry. One upcoming investment or fine detail could provide the extra insight required to close a deal, but even general knowledge of their company or sector could impress a lead."[64]

---

[64] National Association of Sales Professionals. "Closing a Deal: Meeting Preparation." Mark Rothwell [Accessed August 2024], https://www.nasp.com/blog/closing-a-deal-meeting-preparation/.

Chapter 9

Analyzing data. Like during our target marketing technique, we can use demographics and behavior patterns to analyze past purchases and buying preferences. While the era of traditional PowerPoint presentations may be evolving, the impact of a well-crafted slide deck remains significant. I often prepare what I playfully call "silly" customized presentations for many clients. The revolution in slide deck technology has transformed how salespeople showcase their offerings, making each presentation more dynamic and engaging.

The additional effort put into personalizing each presentation does more than inform—it makes clients feel valued and special. This personalized touch is crucial because it compels them to listen attentively and, more importantly, act on what they've learned. By effectively blending comprehensive data analysis with creative presentation skills, we can significantly increase the likelihood of a favorable response.

Setting clear goals. Proper preparation also involves setting clear, strategic goals. Have you ever experienced a sales presentation derail as the buyer veers into unrelated issues or past negative situations? Maintaining a clear goal can refocus the discussion. However, sales goals do not always need to be about closing a deal immediately. Sometimes, our aim might be to embark on a discovery mission, where we seek to understand our prospects' business environments more deeply or establish more robust connections. Such goals foster a richer dialogue and build the groundwork for future interactions, enhancing relationships and sales potential. It puts us right in line for the next stage, engagement.

Engagement stage

As business owners or salespeople, we initiate various media strategies to connect with future consumers, using the general idea of initiating a conversation. Wholeheartedly, if I can get someone on a call with me to discuss their problems, I'll be able to adequately describe a solution and get my buyer to convert to a purchaser. To get to the conversion stage, we must initiate conversations through phone calls, emails, social media, marketing mailers, or even face-to-face interactions.

Regarding the psychological approach, we consider what the person on the other side would prefer. We must literally think about how they will respond, how they will be affected, and try to envision it!

Often, salespeople, me included, take the easy road and communicate in the ways we prefer, but with a complete lack of consideration for the other party. Part of creating that limbic resonant experience is making ourselves available on their level, not ours.

Analyzing data. Asking for a preference is one of the simplest methods to research how a customer prefers to be contacted. This may seem like a small matter, but it is of utmost importance today when humans are inundated with countless methods of mass communication. Our lives are constantly inundated with a barrage of emails, spam texts, promotional messages, illegal scams, legitimate offers, and valuable community engagement. Yes, I'm specifically referring to communication through email. During my business trip to Florida a few weeks ago, we took a brief break to make some cold calls. I was utterly taken aback when we secured two appointments immediately with just a phone call. Architects and design firms in south Florida are constantly overwhelmed with requests for construction materials. Their inbox is flooded with countless emails daily, all asking for their attention. The call efficiently skipped irrelevant details and directly reached the source. Right then, I had to analyze data related to psychological solutions. I would get nowhere if my offer wasn't transmitted over the phone or in person. Emails have literally no engagement impact in that market; they aren't a reliable means of communication! Recently, I asked one of the clients, and she explained that they no longer respond to emails, and if they don't see your product in person, it will never be considered for specification.

Perhaps you've noticed that when signing up for a service online, some companies have started asking, "May we email you or call you?" "Which do you prefer?" Exactly to my point, finding out what method of communication works best with the client will help us psychologically build a better strategy.

Setting clear goals. Setting clear goals for each interaction helps maintain focus and ensures that communications are purposeful and directed toward achieving specific outcomes. Whether the goal is to educate about a product, resolve a concern, or close a sale, having a defined objective steers the conversation and keeps both parties aligned.

By actively engaging with potential customers through their preferred channels, analyzing their communication preferences, and setting clear interaction goals, salespeople can significantly improve the effectiveness of their engagement strategies. This tailored approach respects the consumer's preferences and increases the chances of progressing from initial contact to successful conversion.

Conversion stage

The climax. The close begins to take shape when we've established those clear goals, but we've yet to secure the transaction. Effective communication and trust-building activities should have paved the way, complemented by significant offers that align with the buyer's needs and desires. Yet, even at this late stage, the outcome can still be swayed by deeper psychological undercurrents. Relationships and common cognitive biases significantly influence the decision-making process.

A key strategy for navigating this final push is recognizing and addressing common **cognitive biases** influencing buyer behavior. These biases can affect how prospects perceive your offer and make decisions. For instance, the **confirmation bias**, which is "people's tendency to process information that is consistent with existing beliefs,"[65] can lead customers to favor information that confirms their preexisting beliefs, so reinforcing positive brand experiences and benefits throughout the engagement can align with this tendency. Another example is the **scarcity bias**, where people perceive products as more valuable when they are less available; this is the moment we include influences on timing and stock levels. Highlighting the uniqueness or limited availability of an offer can enhance its attractiveness.

---

[65] Encyclopedia Britannica. "Confirmation Bias." Accessed [August 2024]. https://www.britannica.com/science/confirmation-bias.

Analyzing data. Continuously analyzing customer data throughout the sales process provides invaluable insights that can be leveraged later during the conversion stage. Understanding previous interactions, preferences, and responses allows for a **tailored approach** that resonates personally with the buyer. So look back at your notes from the process to find those nuggets of problem-solving that can help push the buyer over any last hills of indecisiveness.

Setting clear goals. At the conversion stage, we need clear, specific goals for each interaction—again, it's not always just about the close! These goals should go beyond simply "making the sale" to establishing a long-term relationship or setting the stage for future upsells. Defining what you aim to achieve in each interaction helps focus your efforts and ensures that your communications and strategies align with these objectives.

Find the close and seal the deal. Effective closing is less about hard selling and more about skillfully aligning all the efforts you've made to this point. Consider these strategies:

Recognizing Closing Signals: Remember active listening? Pay attention to verbal and non-verbal cues. Watch for questions that hint at logistical concerns like delivery timelines, payment terms, or implementation details. These inquiries often suggest that the customer is visualizing ownership or commitment.

Closing cues to listen for:

"How soon can we get started?"
"Is there a payment plan option?"
"What happens next?"

When you hear these, it's often an indication that the buyer is ready to move forward. Reinforce their readiness by confirming their interest with phrases like, *"It sounds like you're ready to take the next step—let's discuss the details so we can get started!"*

Don't forget if you aren't hearing those cues, it's your clue to bring them into the conversation. That my friends is the *order maker* coming from inside you. Take the client to the close.

Using Assumptive Language: Guide the conversation by framing your language as if the decision is a natural next step. Phrases like, *"When you choose this package..."* or *"After you're on board..."* help create a mental image of the prospect already enjoying the benefits of your offer.

Revisiting and Validating Goals: Bring the conversation back to the customer's initial goals and motivations. Reiterate how your solution aligns with these goals, emphasizing the key pain points you addressed. This reinforces the value you provide and reassures them that their concerns have been met.

"Earlier, you mentioned that streamlining your workflow is a top priority. This plan will help you achieve exactly that by..."

Offering a Choice, Not a Decision: Rather than asking if they want to proceed, offer choices that subtly move towards a commitment. For instance, *"Would you like to start with the basic package or the premium option that includes additional support?"* Giving options can alleviate pressure and empowers the customer to feel in control of the decision.

Creating Urgency without Pressure: Emphasize the value of acting sooner rather than later. Urgency can be established gently by tying decisions to external factors like limited availability or special promotions, but always avoid pressure tactics.

"This offer includes an additional setup bonus for those who enroll by the end of the week. Let's make sure you don't miss out on that advantage."

Addressing Final Objections Gracefully: Any lingering concerns at this point need to be approached with empathy and confidence. Rather than directly challenging their objection, validate it and then redirect their focus to a previously agreed-upon goal or benefit.

"I understand that the budget is a concern, especially with your other investments. Given that this solution can reduce your operational costs in the long run, does this address your concerns?"

Creating a Soft Close: Sometimes, introducing a soft close—a smaller, less risky commitment—can pave the way to the final close. This could be something as simple as signing up for a trial, agreeing to a follow-up meeting with a technical advisor, or even securing a preferred delivery date.

In the final stage, focus on **confidence** and **reinforcement**. Go back to the reason the client contacted your company or walked through the door. Continue to exude confidence in your commitment to their success and show them your enthusiasm in finding the solution to their dilemma. All the while, keep in mind to end and close on a positive note. Finally, use those clearly set goals to outline exactly how the next steps will follow. The result will be an emotionally intelligent close that sets expectations for the outcome to come to light. Whew! Doesn't that sound easy? It's not, it takes practice, but with practice, you can develop that intuition I keep talking about making the process easier over time.

Conclusion

Emotional intelligence profoundly impacts the sales process, emphasizing the imperative role of understanding and responding to clients' emotional cues and needs. This human-centric approach is not merely an addition to sales strategies—it is essential for forming genuine connections that go beyond immediate transactions and cultivate long-term loyalty and repeat business.

Throughout this chapter, we explored how active listening, establishing expertise, empathy, managing reactivity, body language, and creating customized experiences enable sales professionals to navigate the complex dynamics of human interaction. By leveraging these key principles, you can shift from a transactional approach to one that is transformative, fostering deep, resonant connections with clients.

As we move forward, we'll explore the other side of the equation: the psychology behind consumer purchasing decisions. Understanding why and how buyers make choices is how we will refine our approach further proactively assume the sale. By merging insights into buyer psychology with the principles of emotional intelligence, you can create sales strategies that not only resonate with your clients but also influence their decision-making at a deeper level. Let's dive into what drives consumer choices and learn how to harness that knowledge to enhance your sales outcomes.

CHAPTER 10
The Human Element
Buyer Psychology

You might think that buyer psychology is *old school* and even say, "Come on, Alison, this is basic sales stuff." Well, my friends, this is foundational beginning "stuff." When I begin working with any client, I determine in the first few conversations whether the client has that salesperson's intuition or if it's yet to be uncovered. If you are an entrepreneur or a salesperson, you have intuition. My job is to find it!

Some folks come up with a business plan, without realizing they sell with a reactive mindset. Perhaps you've come across a friend in business with a knack for business but lacks a knack for people?

Growing up, my father talked a lot about his older brother's inability to succeed in school. He was a terrible student in his teen years but went on to create a corporation in the fifties which eventually became a multi-million-dollar company later purchased by Cintas Corporation[66]. My uncle is a perfect example of a man with a plan, but you'll have to take my word for it, he did not have a knack for people, nor authority. Great business mind, terrible sales skills.

My goal is to help you see the motivators behind purchase decisions, advertising and the marketing! I want to encourage you to refine those consumer purchase instincts and train that intuition regardless of your natural selling abilities. **Remember, everyone is capable of learning to sell, intuition is a big part of that development.**

As we discussed in the last chapter, emotional intelligence is one thing, but understanding where those body language cues, or empathetic responses are coming from, is another. Understanding these perspectives will help you create better customized experiences and prepare you more for that closing situation by learning to apply what the buyer needs from you, the salesperson.

Understanding people's *why* is the starting point. I like to use a **decision tree** to highlight the emotional triggers which influence consumer buying decisions. Here's an example AI created for me based on one I used in a presentation recently.

---

[66] Cintas Corporation, "About Us," accessed October 28, 2024, https://www.cintas.com/about-us.

BEYOND ORDER MAKERS

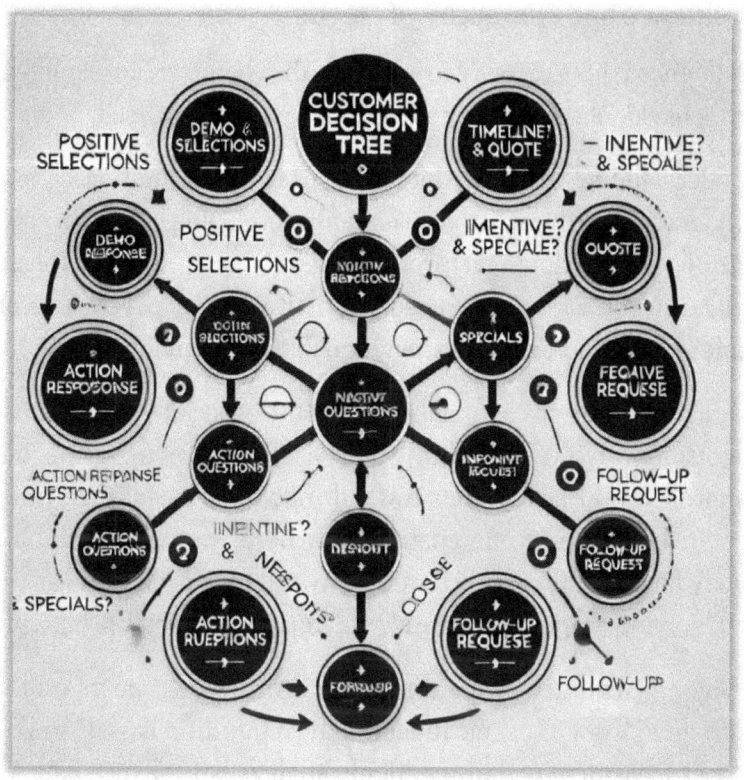

Just like the diagram, I want you to develop connection skills, anticipatory actions, and proactive movements. If you read *The Art of Selling, We Make Order Makers, Not Order Takers*, you might remember my topic "chameleoning. Chameleoning is a perfect example of how we must use all we learned in chapter nine: reading body language, using empathy, establishing expertise, to present and create a sense of community and customization. Let's talk a bit more about influence and how we accomplish that trust through the buyer's psyche.

Chapter 10

Influence and Hierarchy of Needs

Influence is "the capacity to influence the character, development or behavior of someone or something, or the effect itself."[67]

Understanding Maslow's hierarchy of needs is the first step in understanding human behavior and developing effective sales strategies. "Maslow's hierarchy of needs is a psychological theory that categorizes human needs into five levels: **psychological, safety, love and belonging, esteem, and self-actualization.**"[68]

Our *needs* are why we make decisions, especially when those decisions involve spending money. If we are to refine our approach and sales pitch toward individual needs, we must begin by meeting our customers where they are, watching body language, listening for clues to a client's needs, and above all, staying empathetic toward solving a customer's problem.

When a customer walks through our doors or appears on the screen in front of us, we must make an intuition-based, on-the-spot assessment and immediately analyze how we can balance their energy, compliment their style & meet them exactly where they are in that moment! Teaching a direct sales retail or in-home selling employee how to conduct that inspection within seconds is how I make sales superstars. Moving on to perfecting this skillset of observation, let's review why humans make decisions in the first place.

---

[67] Definition of "influence," Merriam-Webster.com, accessed August 02, 2024, https://www.merriam-webster.com/dictionary/influence.

[68] "Exploring Needs And Preferences: Understanding The Market And Consumers" MarketSpotAudit, accessed June 2024, https://www.marketspotaudit.com/consumer-analysis-needs-and-preferences

Physiological needs

Food, water, air, shelter. Our survival instincts. Typically, we categorize purchases like buying a home or buying an air system for our home as part of our physiological needs. Appliances can fall into this category because they directly affect how we store and prepare our food or how we clean our clothes. We can possibly add subliminal assurance purchases like car insurance, extended warranties, or water treatment systems at box stores to this category, although they fall on the border of safety needs. Mattresses, even hotels, fall into this mindset because where we sleep affects our overall health.

Old strategies. Tell them how they will die if they don't do X, essentially selling fear, fear-based solutions, and reactionary purchases. I remember processing these sales techniques to explain the worst-case scenario and convincing someone to value my solution. Salespeople emulate how we will become the knight in shining armor, here to save the day! The fear approach scares buyers into their purchase by placing fear upon the physiological necessities of living. Yuck! Strategies which scare buyers into deciding based on fear factors or survival instincts are simply leveraging the fear, and we want to build trust and loyalty instead.

New strategies. To build trust, focus on active listening and becoming the first call. The opposite of fear is guiding trust. Using expertise as a guide, if we slow down and build stronger relationships with our clients, based on honest experience and without pushing toward a decision but allowing the client to come to an informed decision, we will become a trusted resource. It's more likely that we will build sustainable relationships with a high probability of referrals, while also having a good chance of increasing our notoriety within our community. This is not being the smartest person in the room either! It is staying humble, possibly inserting a pause in the sale stating: "I need to look into X further and get back to you". New strategies focus on building trust, if necessary, showing the research available to prove why our solution is recommended.

Safety needs

Individuals seek safety and security in their purchases. Whether it's physical safety, financial security, or health and well-being, people look for products or services that provide protection, stability, and longevity, ultimately creating a sense of belonging and assurance. Think about how healthcare, pharmaceuticals, financial institutions, and legal services advertise—often focusing on how their offerings will keep us safe and secure.

Old strategies. Old and outdated is the approach to selling safety, leaning heavily on exaggeration of circumstances which leads to emotional manipulation. Whenever we see advertisements showcasing *skinny, happy, glowing* people living exciting lives after using a product, this implies if we aren't jumping toward this bandwagon, we might be missing out. Like other fear-based tactics, you might see aggressive tactics, like *loud attorneys* screaming promises of bringing justice to victims, or pharmaceutical ads where *dancing, happy people* are suddenly cured thanks to a new treatment. These visuals tap directly into fear-based selling, focusing on worst-case scenarios and insecurities—"If you don't use this, you're at risk!" These old strategies use fear to push buyers into quick, reactive purchases.

New strategies. A proactive approach to selling based on someone's need for safety and security also goes back to building trust and creating feelings of empowerment. Advertising toward women has improved tremendously in this area. For instance: if you've seen any of the video ads built to sell these new waist-cinching swimsuits, they contain beautiful, strong-looking women who are not stick figures, and many are eating ice cream while riding horses and wearing new waist-cinching swimsuits. Instead of selling based on fear and insecurity, this company TA3[69] focuses on body positivity with an undercurrent of "I don't care what you think of me" power.

Summing up Safety, I'll tell a story familiar to most of my readers that sums up the safety selling techniques.

Purchasing a home without an inspection.

As a real estate agent, our job is to not only find the *perfect* homes for our clients, but also to guide our buyers through the closing process. One of the hardest parts of closing residential real estate deals is getting through the inspection process of a property. Already under a contract, inspections make or break sales contracts. One way an effective sales leader manages this process is by staying close to the prospective buyer or seller during this process and acting as an advocate for their respective parties.

In 2020, I noticed a trend in real estate edging purchasers away from home inspection to increase their odds in securing a contract. Agents recommended prospective buyers to make purchase offers with contingencies avoiding inspection. This is one evolutional sales strategy I can't get behind. As both a sales

---

[69] https://ta3swim.com/

trainer or as someone working around construction and remodeling, never purchase a home without an inspection and if I had my license today, I would sell myself as an agent with *safety advocacy* even if it meant losing a few contracts up front. Using legal assistance and creative contract writing I couldn't play the game if it meant giving up my client's inspection rights to their new home prior to ratifying the contract. There is simply just too much at risk by buying blind for the average homeowner.

Love and belonging

These needs revolve around social connections, relationships, and belonging to a community. An emotional need innate within most humans is a desire to be a part of, receive love, and give in return.

Old strategies. Aspirational branding, like Ralph Lauren or Disney World, as described in the first section. I remember early television ads used visuals of belonging to a group or a club, encouraging the buyer to "join in." Picture brand visuals or sales pitches promoting community, social interactions, personal relationships, and interpersonal reflection. Nonprofits are a great example; even those awful commercials with the pets in despair pull at our heartstrings to donate and "join in."

New strategies. In today's selling strategies, social media is everything. We all know that, but we can never know for how long; however, one thing is for sure: the videography is here to stay. As was mentioned in previous chapters, TikTok and the use of influencer programs is the new Amazon shopping experience. Sellers depend upon video testimonials and reviews in order to appeal to our pillar one, the aspirational pillar. Often, many of these video reviews, testimonials, and or influencers with sponsored content are entering our feeds based on an algorithm with a pre-programmed notion that we will be interested in hearing what this ad has to say. Companies are hiring individuals from everyday life to share their experiences and are breaking down the barriers of stardom and impossible-to-reach aspirations. By making the aspirational reach a little "closer to home" companies are appealing to an entire generation through a new set of "belonging needs." It's a little scary because the influencer, truthful or not, can make or break a purchase.

Esteem needs

Parallel to love and belonging, we achieve a level of self-respect, achievement, and recognition. Esteem typically involves luxury goods, status symbols, and products or services offering a sense of accomplishment.

Old strategies. Level-up brands like Ralph Lauren, Tommy Hilfiger, FUBU, and even Nike Air Jordans come to mind and hit this emotional level. Selling products using movie stars and influencers highlighting idealistic and unachievable status references was a way to meet our esteem needs. Another one of the oldest tricks in the books is simply to place a higher price tag on an item regardless of its cost per unit and pay someone to write an article about it. Have you ever accidentally purchased something because you perceived it to be of exceptional quality and value simply because of the price? I have. Most recently, that misperception happened while buying sheets online. I read an article on the *New York Times Wirecutter*[70]

---

[70] https://www.nytimes.com/wirecutter/blog/sleeping-on-2000-sheets/

discussing the value of sleeping in expensive sheets, and I must admit knowing what I know about PR, Wirecutter is basically a paid advertisement section of the NYT in the form of an informative piece. But, alas, I'm reading about the whys I should get one and my mouth is watering to try a set, so I cringe and order the least expensive option. Once arrived I'm sad to report I've also purchased sheets from a department store that matched this quality so I'm going to chalk this experience up to great esteem advertising to which I fell for it hook, line, and sinker.

New strategies. Somewhat tied into the aspirational strategies of love and belonging, esteem needs involve consumers relying on rock stars, movie stars, and celebrities for influence. Esteem requires an affluent celebrity, even though today's influencers could easily be your next-door neighbor with 1.7 million likes on TikTok. Based on Generation Z and Generation Alpha's current statistics, we will seemingly rely upon video testimonials to appeal to esteem for some time. I like to get my clients the biggest bang for their buck and maximize their budget by selling through esteem. I do this by tailoring and creating product and pricing tiers and adding priority discounts or special offers for specific clientele making it easy to hit the esteem button without having to fork over money for an influencer. Relaying the message of customization strongly influences esteem purchases, without the esteem price tag and without the expensive PR article.

Self-Actualization

At the top of Maslow's hierarchy, self-actualization is the desire to reach one's fullest potential! The laws of nature encourage us to engage in meaningful activities. Products and services that inspire us to be creative, achieve a new level of personal growth, or engage in unaltered self-expression cater to these needs.

Old strategies. When I contemplate the history of entrepreneurs and branding associated with this hierarchy, I think of cults and the propulsion of fake leaders in our world who draw in an audience of people based upon some belief that they are helping society in some form or fashion. On a positive note, I fondly remember the Save the Manatees campaign from the early '90s or the Save the Animal commercials on television. Those poor "ugly cute" mammals in Florida gained so much support and advocacy simply from the appeal to our gut instincts to save the planet. Those flashy poor animal advertisements make me want to get involved, to try and heal the world, and above all, they make us want to make a difference, and typically with a little push from a classic folk star like Jimmy Buffett, helps too.[71] Another example that is still working for the company today is the ASPCA with their ad campaigns showing the neglect and poor care for animals across our nation. Sadly, the commercials are unbearable for me to watch, but as a contributor to the group, it worked, and it still can, but is that who we want to be, and doesn't this type of advertising also cross over into the fear factor too? Is that the vision we would want to present? Let me show you just how ugly it can get so that you can feel better about yourself by sending us $25 a month from the comfort of your couch.

New strategies. While we still want to save the planet, a bold way of showing a new strategy toward self-actualization is by

---

[71] Save the Manatee Club. "Our Vision and Mission." Accessed August 2, 2024. https://savethemanatee.org/about/our-vision-and-mission/.

embracing and publicly addressing topics which might have held a hush-hush attitude in the past. For example, the concept of embracing mental health is a contemporary subject, and psychological services, addiction treatment centers, and similar entities have an underlying sales component. Perhaps part of this "new" strategy is simply the embracing of unorthodox subject matter and the lack of fear of judgement by society.

Consider the way YouTube has transformed into a vast repository of self-improvement resources. If there's anything we want to learn, and I mean absolutely anything, you can bet there's a video about it on YouTube. My goal is to showcase and tweak your actions or "methods" of achieving limbic resonance and utilizing emotional intelligence during sales.

To continue this psychological sales journey, we must consider two perspectives: the consumer purchase and the salesperson's selling journeys.

Consumer Journey

Awareness, consideration, and decision. Let's briefly walk through our buyer's **"when"** and decision-making stages and their consumer journey.

Awareness stage

This is the initial moment a consumer engages in the thought process of making a purchase. For some of us, this could be walking the dog and remembering to reorder food. It's that moment when we come home to a hot house and realize the HVAC needs repair or replacement. It's walking into the kitchen and seeing a time-worn sink and countertop starting to show failure. It's purchasing a new home, realizing how much we hate carpet, and recognizing that we must replace the floors. It's driving down the road and seeing a car or truck we'd rather own instead of the one in the shop at this very moment. From small to large purchases, a moment clicks within a consumer—triggering them to explore more details about a purchase.

The goal: Ignite a moment—a spark. Capture Attention.

The action: We must get in front of our decision-makers and present why we are there for their "time of need." I will also note that the "time of need" fluctuates.

> **Pro tip**—In this social media era, we typically have only three to eight seconds to steal a viewer's attention online, so keep that in mind when formulating an online video ad or pitch.

Consideration stage

Sometimes, when I teach a showroom or retail salesperson, I wish they recognized the importance of the consideration stage. Once awareness is converted to interest, a consumer enters the consideration stage. Consideration is the precise moment consumers deliberate on options, compare alternatives, and weigh the pros and cons.

Recognizing the importance of this stage is vital in a retail or showroom environment. When customers walk through the door, they are usually past the point of mere curiosity and considering a purchase. They might be seeking additional information, hoping to see the product in person, or ready to decide. It's not enough for salespeople to merely be present;

they must be proactive, knowledgeable, and persuasive. They must guide the consumer, provide valuable insights, and help tilt the decision to favor their offerings.

In a wholesale selling environment, it's the salesperson's job to bring products to our buyers' attention—to bring the intimacy of a retail selling environment to their doors or just to the wholesale counter! We have become an order maker by merchandising our products in clients' retail outlets. We don't wait for them to ask; we take the time to look for what they need and bring it to their attention before they even know they need such items.

The simple principle behind this is, *"We Make Order Makers, Not Order Takers."* Please don't wait for consideration to walk in our door; instead, bring awareness and respect to your customers' doors.

The challenge I present to my readers is knowing what we need to sell and relaying it to customers' psychological needs, engaging them in a way that produces influence in an honest, transparent, not "grabby" manner. At that point, we have now created a limbic resonant environment.

Remember all the brand work in the first section? Our sales pitches and consideration techniques directly form from our UVP statements, and then we employ emotional intelligence to create solutions and present them to the audience.

The goal: Successfully transition a buyer from the awareness to the consideration stage.

The action: Use emotional intelligence to read subtle cues that indicate what the customer is looking for and how ready they are to proceed. Adapting the sales approach to match the customer's pace and decision-making process can significantly increase the likelihood of a sale.

Decision stage

At this stage in the buyer's journey, the consumer is ready with data and preparing to sift through the information they've gathered to make a well-informed decision. Typically, this involves creating a mental or documented list of pros and cons. By this point, we, as sales professionals, have presented our proposal, sent a quote, or made an offer.

During this comparison period, the consumer meticulously evaluates the options. I've always championed follow-up as a strategic move in this very moment to remain front and center in the customer's mind. We must recognize that the buyer may have already leaned toward a decision. Influencing the final choice hinges on the finer details, and it's not over yet!

> ***The goal:*** *To ensure all details—additional benefits, superior service, or unmatched quality—set our offering apart, pushing the client in a final direction, positive or negative.*
>
> ***The action(s):*** *Listen and ask questions, as this is vital at this stage to produce a favorable response in our pending consumer mindset.*

Include follow-up as part of this stage. As salespeople, we can use follow-up to transform a customer from the consideration stage to the decision stage by simply reminding them we are waiting for a decision! We reinforce the value of our proposal, address any last-minute concerns, and tip the decision scale in our favor through thoughtful engagement and precise communication. We'll talk more about active listening here for a bit.

Knowing **why** our consumers purchase from us, we can better determine **how** we will accomplish this and correlate it to our brand.

Conclusion

Understanding buyer psychology is far from being old-school salesmanship; it's foundational to building effective and lasting relationships. The key to this lies in honing your intuition to better read the emotional cues and motivations behind consumer decisions. Developing this seller's intuition is not an overnight journey—it requires practice, active engagement, and empathy.

We explored how the hierarchy of needs impacts purchasing behavior and why adapting our strategies to align with these needs is critical. By moving beyond outdated fear-based tactics and embracing trust-building techniques, we can create authentic relationships with our clients. This approach is about being proactive and empathetic, tailoring our sales pitches to meet the psychological and emotional needs of our customers.

Ultimately, when we understand and connect with our clients on a deeper level, we don't just close sales—we form genuine bonds that foster loyalty and increase the likelihood of repeat business and referrals. This ability to read between the lines and balance the psychological and emotional cues is what separates good sales professionals from great ones.

As we move forward, remember that achieving success in sales isn't just about perfecting our techniques or understanding buyer psychology—it's also about maintaining a healthy balance between our professional and personal lives. In the next chapter, we'll explore the importance of work-life balance and its impact on long-term success and well-being. After all, the key to thriving in sales and beyond lies in achieving a harmonious blend of ambition and self-care. Let's dive into how we can cultivate that balance while pursuing professional excellence.

CHAPTER 11
Humanizing Mentality
A Work-Life Balance Conversation

Humanizing "work-life balance" begins with manifesting rebounds and making space for new ideas to come to fruition. We must learn how to breathe and create space for change. After COVID-19, I felt the burn, the burden. This burden led me on a path to re-inventing and self-improving, finding new coping mechanisms, and changing my perspective on how much time I dedicate to not only work but also self-care, as self-care and faith became my new priorities. The youngest generations are seemingly more aware than ever of putting self-care first. I wish we had this type of education earlier in my childhood, teenage years, and yes, even a course during college could have prevented some of my own challenges I finally had to deal with later in life.

Burnout is a trending possibility among sales professionals, entrepreneurs, small business owners, and yes, even C-suite professionals.

The entrepreneur has added stresses of financial insecurity, finding and making sales, keeping inventory checks and balances, managing creative processes, and sometimes just getting up and going every day. Thus, the human element in sales and our mental state are as important as ever as we navigate the uncertainty of life and businesses with outside forces like government, logistics, inflation, upper management.

We face issues with our children, family, and people, places, and things we cannot control but must navigate swimmingly to push forward. The old adage "sink or swim" is the most real for the entrepreneur, and I can attest to pushing through one day at a time and finding success, with balance.

In the last five years I decided to incorporate the following ideals to improve my work-life balance. Over time they continue to improve my confidence and execution "wearing multiple hats", like most small business owners.

Finding work-life balance and improving our mental consciousness is not just a dream but also a tangible reality. So, let's dive into these familiar and unfamiliar topics: **time management, social media planning, setting boundaries, stress management with mindfulness and meditation, music, physical activity,**

hobbies, and sabbaticals. These are not just ideas; they are tools we can use to take control of our lives.

Managing stress and prioritizing mental health are vital aspects of overall well-being, particularly in the fast-paced sales world.

Time Management

We're going to get to a deep dive on time management in the next chapter, but I want to briefly touch on it in this chapter to drive home the point: **mastering effective time-management techniques and understanding the significance of establishing boundaries to cater to your needs beyond work is the foundation for a good work-life balance**. It doesn't just save you time, good time management will reduce stress.

Later in chapter twelve I'll review with you, **time blocking**, allocating specific time slots for tasks allows for focused attention. It minimizes the anxiety often caused by looming deadlines, creating a space to complete our tasks, which reduces stress.

Integrating **deliberate breaks** is another key aspect of my time-management strategy, which aims to enhance mindfulness. These breaks are sanctuaries, providing opportunities to detach, reflect, and recharge. Whether stepping outside for a walk or simply enjoying a muted moment away from screens, these pauses are vital for mental clarity and overall well-being.

Experiment with these time-management techniques to find what best suits your lifestyle. Whether it's meticulously planning each task or setting aside guarded moments for breaks, the goal is to create a balanced routine that fosters productivity and personal well-being. Embrace these practices to cultivate mindfulness, reduce stress, and achieve a harmonious work-life balance.

Setting Boundaries

I laugh a little, talking about boundaries, and as a natural people pleaser and customer service guru, the thought of saying no terrifies me! However, boundaries are crucial to managing stress and prioritizing mental health. Boundaries are guidelines or limits we establish to protect our well-being and maintain a healthy work-life balance. These can include

- Setting limits on work-related activities outside designated hours, such as checking emails or taking calls
- Saying no to tasks or commitments when necessary
- Delegating responsibilities
- Asserting our right to privacy and personal time by setting aside time for it and honoring that

Americans are the worst at taking time for us. On trips to Canada and south Florida, I found that other cultures prioritize work-life balance better than others. For instance, Quebec and Miami have a culture of taking and having lunch! The audacity! Every time I planned to visit accounts and network with design and architectural professionals in these cities, I had to allow for space for lunch. I experienced pushback if I attempted to meet during those precious 12–1 p.m. hours. What a concept! Take your lunch, and don't work through it. Is it possible? Try it yourself and put away the phone. Can you do it?

"Saying no doesn't have to be rude or confrontational; it can be done politely but firmly," [72] according to Business Tech Weekly. Establishing clear boundaries with colleagues, clients, family, and supervisors is another necessary element to prevent burnout and maintain our mental and emotional well-being. One example is declaring the hours you are willing to take phone calls or answer emails. When I first started my career in NYC, I would speak to the agents in Hong Kong or answer emails from my Blackberry all hours of the night. Was this necessary? Did I need to be so "important" to respond to those inquiries? No. I was wrong. It took years to break this habit of giving away my time to make myself look more critical and responsive! Later in life, as a salesperson, I still needed to respond quickly, assertively, and as soon as possible! After all, getting back to sales leads or inquiries is fundamental. But over the years, I've learned to slow down a bit, and one of my essential techniques is making a phone call from an email inquiry or a text. The best sales strategy I've developed is not responding to a written request with a written request! Instead, I find that connecting in person establishes boundaries with the client. If it's outside of my working hours and I'm in my time priority space, I will respond to a text inquiry stating that I will get back to them first thing in the morning. Emails must be left cold until I've logged in to review them. I will call the client to review their needs and let them know I'll get back to them tomorrow with the answer/offer/required information.

An interior designer friend of mine in Washington, D.C. had homeowners pushing her time boundaries regularly. Brook was young in business and often had clients texting and calling

---

[72] Business Tech Weekly. "5 Strategies for Working Smarter, Not Harder." Accessed June 2024.
https://www.businesstechweekly.com/productivity/automation/working smarter/.

from 8–9 p.m. She would respond to and engage with these client inquiries immediately. After all, her clients were working "Washingtonians"; they put in their twelve-hour days better than anyone in the country. And their home renovation project required attention, no matter the time of day! One evening she was hanging out with me when she took one of these calls, and I waited patiently as she took the call from a desperate homeowner to discuss their drapery dilemma. After she finished the call, I asked her about the emergency, and when she exclaimed how the client had no perception of work-life balance and respect for her time, I quietly asked her why she allowed the client to run her schedule. Brook and I bantered for a while about boundaries and the necessity of setting them up with our clients from the inception. Clients will run us to the ground if we allow them to do so. We must set those boundaries from the inception of our relationship and do our best to hold them where possible.

Engaging in Mindfulness and Meditation

What are your practices for **stress management**? Do you practice **mindfulness**? **Meditation**? "Mindfulness involves being fully present in the moment and paying attention to your thoughts, feelings, and sensations without judgement. This can be done through activities such as meditation, deep breathing exercises, or simply taking a few moments to focus on your senses."[73]

According to the Harvard Business Review, Google prides itself on being socially conscious, offering employees substantial benefits and perks, including over a dozen mindfulness

---

[73]Health Centre NZ, accessed September 25, 2024, https://healthcentre.nz/the-power-of-self-care-empowering-women-to-prioritize-themselves.

courses. Google's most popular mindfulness course, "Search Inside Yourself," [74] offered since 2007, has thousands of alumni. Google believes these mindfulness programs teach EI, which helps people better understand their colleagues' motivations. They also boost resilience to stress and improve mental focus. Participants of the "Search Inside Yourself" program report being calmer, more patient, and better able to listen. They also say the program helped them better handle stress and defuse emotions.

Keeping a weekly task list that includes mindfulness, and meditation helps me balance professional responsibilities with personal activities. This organized approach ensures I dedicate ample time to work and leisure, contributing to a fulfilling life. Planning with realistic goals allows for a smoother transition between work and personal time, reducing the likelihood of work spillover and ensuring I have dedicated time for relaxation and connection with loved ones.

As a former workaholic who used to perform at top speed, my life has changed dramatically since leaving corporate positions. While remaining very structured during scheduled work hours, even working from home, high-performing workaholics find sitting still for five minutes, let alone thirty minutes, challenging.

Small moments of meditation help during times of stress, even as little as three minutes make a difference in how we feel. I can practice sitting with my eyes closed and breathing, and

---

[74] Gelles, David. "Why Google, Target, and General Mills Are Investing in Mindfulness." *Harvard Business Review*, December 2015. https://hbr.org/2015/12/why-google-target-and-general-mills-are-investing-in-mindfulness.

Chapter 11

something interesting for me has been watching the colors that present themselves while still.

Once when I was incredibly stressed at work, I sat in the car for five minutes to decompress. Taking moments to breathe through stressful work can make working with others easier. The stress of doing business can and will affect our lives. It's up to us to find peace and calm amid it all. Over the years, close friends have seen me find peace and relaxation through yoga. Yoga is an exercise that includes stretching. Stretching exercises can help reduce the mental and physical stress caused by constantly being busy. I make it a point to do these exercises daily to relax my back, calves, and other tense muscles that result from sitting in the car for long periods. People often think commitment to something like yoga requires too much effort. I was one of those people.

After all, it's challenging to find time for these moments in our active lives. Even if you only have ten minutes, it's valuable.

You don't have to dedicate huge blocks of time. Before I realized this, I was concerned with my apparel, my mat, the time to get to the studio, and the time it would take to finish the class, shower, and resume life. As an overachiever, of course, I was taking the ninety-minute hot yoga class, which in total required almost three hours of my day. Why couldn't I open my eyes and see that a simple ten minutes of stretching at home, with no gear, no mat, no car, no studio, would benefit me just as much as the giant huge commitment I pursued? After moving to my cozy townhome near a beautiful lake, I started appreciating the benefits of leisurely walks and using the environment to be mindful. No equipment necessary!

Music for mindfulness

One of my favorites is Insight Timer. It's a free app from any phone store. There are others; I've seen Calm and Breathe. Of course, thousands of mindfulness videos are readily available on YouTube. It's simply a matter of taking the time to find those moments to use these apps and videos.

One practical innovation in the new age is **music frequency.**

Classical, natural sounds and even video game music can all affect our brains, causing them to rewire and create new focus. By tuning in, we tune out the cloudiness created by stress.

Music can have a profound effect on both the emotions and the body. Faster music can make you feel more alert and concentrate better. Upbeat music can make you feel more optimistic about life. A slower tempo can mute your mind and relax your muscles, making you feel soothed while releasing the day's stress. Music is effective for relaxation and stress management.

Research confirms these firsthand experiences with music. Current findings indicate that music around sixty beats per minute can cause the brain to synchronize with the beat, causing alpha brainwaves (frequencies from 8–14 hertz or cycles per second). This alpha brainwave is what is present when we are relaxed and conscious. To induce sleep (a delta brainwave of five hertz), a person may need to devote at least forty-five minutes in a comfortable position, listening to calming music. Music can profoundly affect emotions and the body. According to the University of Nevada, "Researchers at Stanford University have said that listening to music can change brain functioning to the same extent as medication."[75] They noted that anybody can access music, making it an easy stress-reduction tool.

I encourage anyone looking for simple ways to make slight changes in their daily stress relief practices by simply tuning into these specific music genres. Whether playing them on the showroom floor, in the car, or at your desk, watch how they affect you, and tune into the one that helps you find that reconnect.

Getting Physically Active

Being active is the number one doctor-recommended stress reliever, but who has the time? All it takes is thirty minutes a day to clear your mind. It's one of the reasons I have dogs; they force me to get out in nature and take those needed walks to clear my mind of fluff and clutter. As a former athlete, I've stepped away from super fit focus and stressing over getting to the gym. As I've aged, finding time for a simple walk two to three times a day helps me get back to reality and out of stress mode. Not to mention the benefits of light exercise and movement for creating ideas and sparking creativity.

Have you ever gotten in the car, and your mind starts exploding into ideas and crafting plans? This change of scenery can move

---

[75] University of Nevada, Reno. "Releasing Stress Through the Power of Music." Virtual Relaxation Room. Accessed June 18th, 2024. https://www.unr.edu/counseling/virtual-relaxation-room/releasing-stress-through-the-power-of-music.

me out of stale mode and into action planning. So, if leads are feeling silent, dry or dead, it's time for me to get in the car, find a trail, and go walking/hiking. By the time my journey is complete, my mind feels regenerated.

Engaging in Hobbies and Activities

We must have **hobbies and activities** to keep us mentally sane! I have found that employers who incorporate physical activity among "the team" have the best "team attitude" across all employees. Let your hair down and find some memorable times at least monthly to get your employees or coworkers out for a game of golf, bowling, beach volleyball, roller skating (yes, it's making a comeback), or other activities. Promoting work-life balance in the workplace starts from the top. One of my favorite hobbies for finding balance is cooking. I love to come home and pull random ingredients out of the fridge like I'm on an episode of *Chopped* and see what I can create—chopping vegetables, simmering something braising on the stove-top, or the excitement of heating my outdoor pizza oven, making the dough, and deciding what toppings will be featured on my "kitchen sink" pizza. Inviting a friend to partake in my latest inventions lets me escape the day-to-day stresses, financial insecurities, or pressure to succeed. I invite you to consider what hobby takes you to that place of aloneness and complete efficiency. Doing puzzles is a grand idea, like painting, gardening, or building something. All successful hobbies transport us to a different space and mindset.

Chapter 11

Taking a Sabbatical

As an entrepreneur, taking a sabbatical is a decision of one. There is no corporate rule on when and if this should happen. A sabbatical can be a week, a month, or a time when work and everything work-related shut down completely. For me, I ensure my short sabbaticals involve minimal digital equipment. No social media, phones, or email, but I've allowed old-fashioned movies on DVD. It's a time to be alone with myself and my thoughts. In the last three years, I've rented a house in a remote location on an island in North Carolina called Ocracoke.

Friends of mine in Richmond split a house off-season. We go in November when everything shuts down and the island comes to a complete halt. Most restaurants are closed, and there is no traffic, but the weather is mild. It isn't winter yet, and fall is still turning over. The island is only 2.5 miles long, so we get around on rented bicycles and drive to the mile-wide beachfront to sit in the sun while the calm wind blows our stresses away. I've visited this island when it still feels like summer and sometimes when it feels like winter, but the weather doesn't matter. We've almost zero internet connection, enough in an absolute emergency, and we bring enough groceries to cook every meal in the rented house. Dogs are free, people are free, and no media! Seven days of this is enough sabbatical for me to clear my brain. It's a real vacation: no water parks, no mini golf, no significant activities at all, just time to read, relax, and, for me, cook and feed friends. This time each year creates space for stress to leave and an open mind to wander in. Meditations during sunrise and laughter at night fill the void of worrying about what's next or what needs to be. Our society is filling vacations with stuff: stuff to do, places to be, people to see, places to be seen, cruises full of nightlife, bars to enjoy, chefs to try, and more. I would need a vacation from those styles of vacations, and those are optional. Another idea for a sabbatical is to tour a country you've never seen. Don't sign up for silly tours; don't buy tickets to the museum. Just rent a bike and go around and look at the people and the buildings, eat the food, and just be alone. This type of sabbatical allows one to meet new people, step outside of a comfort zone, and learn about a culture with zero outside influence from a spouse, friend, or partner with their own opinions. Have you ever read *Eat, Pray, Love*? This old classic is a perfect example of someone experiencing burnout from life and choosing to take the deadness inside and turn it upside down. The author found a new path and balance by exploring other cultures and taking it alone. Experiencing burnout from life and stresses of work, decisions, chosen paths, etc., can be changed; we must find the space and allow ourselves moments of aloneness to experience real change. The biggest point is taking the time to find your sabbatical. What will that look like? It doesn't have to cost tons of money, it doesn't have to involve air or significant car travel. Above all, find that time and secure it, and don't take no for an answer, even when it's yourself thinking of changing the plan to relax.

Conclusion

Achieving work-life balance and prioritizing mental health are decisive, needful endeavors for all of us. We can reduce stress and enhance productivity by simply saying yes to the time for ourselves. It's difficult to accept **we are the primary cause of imbalance in our lives. We are also the primary source in our resistance to change.**

Chapter 11

Setting clear boundaries will envelop a safeguarding for personal well-being and preventing burnout, whether establishing limits on work-related communications or prioritizing self-care activities.

Additionally, incorporating hobbies, physical activities, and regular breaks into daily life can promote relaxation and rejuvenation. Finally, the concept of sabbaticals offers a valuable opportunity to disconnect from work and reconnect with oneself, providing much-needed perspective and renewal. By implementing these strategies, sales professionals and entrepreneurs can cultivate a healthier, more balanced lifestyle while achieving sustainable success.

> ### Case study #1

Showroom staff in a tile distribution and custom stone showroom.

While completing a workshop with the sales staff, I heard over and over the same complaints: We have no time for anything extra, and we work from 7 a.m. to 4 p.m. with a constant flow of showroom traffic. We have no time in the day for outreach and can barely get our quotes out in time. We sometimes need help maintaining the appearance of the showroom or changing out sample displays because we need to catch up on how busy we are all the time. Busy. We are all busy. Processing this dilemma for this business was easy for me, but it took time for staff to accept and look for change. The owner and I then worked on a customized solution to move into appointments for designers and specific days each staff could dedicate to their design meeting days.

Controlling and changing the flow of walk-in traffic is a third-party element which takes time to move. After all, we can't control other people's time and motivation for entering a store, nor should we push away from business! So instead find set days of the week for each staffer to dedicate to their accounts and in a quiet space to think, knowing other staff are available to meet with walk-in traffic.

Setting the tone for moving this beast into motion takes time, deep thinking, and initiative-taking scheduling for sales staff. The "off the floor" staff can use this precious time to execute follow-up, process and execute necessary research for customized project orders, process quotes, analyze sales data, and craft outreach lists to ensure they stay in front of their clients and keep them on top of their minds. To be concise and clear, showroom staff need the time "off the floor," which can be blocked in one, two, or three-hour increments once or twice a week. Dedicating two full workdays a week utilizing appointment systems like Acuity or Calendly to ensure that when clients call for an appointment or the staff needs to make an appointment, they have a minimum of two or three full eight-hour days dedicated to lengthy consultations. Client meetings can last thirty minutes or three hours, depending on the project. How much confidence can a relaxed environment create when employees know they have dedicated time for working and processing in a calm work environment?

Chapter 11

Case study #2

An entrepreneur who owns a less forward-facing service to the public.

Her business model is 80 percent B2B and 20 percent B2C. Like the previous business, I heard similar comments about lack of time: I don't have time to sell; I don't have time for client outreach, and I need help when I come in on Mondays and get stuck in my emails for over half of the day. I still need follow-up emails with clients. People have told me I'm too slow in responding to their emails, or they tell me I didn't respond at all. While these are different issues from the previous case study, they have a similar root cause: overall lack of time management.

My work with the client started with breaking down her work week to find time slots for her to create lists to prepare her for Monday's workload on Friday. Her final effort before she closes out for the week is to organize her emails. She was filing away the items in her inbox, flagging items that required follow-up, and listing to-do lists for execution on Monday morning. The simple time block for Friday afternoons—in her case, an entire half-day—had to be dedicated to follow-through, not just follow-up. Also, we put into play a method of replying to emails that come through during the week with an estimated response time, creating expectations for clients' needs. That way, once she responded to the request, she could drag it into one of her time blocks for executing drawings, creating invoices, calling customers, and more. After some simple blocking out time during the week for each specific task at hand—accounting, design execution (her service), client appointment days, community outreach and B2B relationship hours, and email follow-through and list creations—my client told me she felt a breath of fresh air. She felt as if she was walking in new shoes. She now had control over the business management tasks and could breathe through tasks and customer expectations. What a relief for both her and me.

Case study #3

Procrastinate anyone?

An author attempts to write a forty-thousand-word book. Procrastination overwhelms her.

Ha, it's no secret: this third case study is mine! Hi, my name is procrastination; it's nice to meet you! Yes, manifestation selling can work even for creatives lost in procrastination and delay tactics. Authoring a forty-thousand-word book was complicated for me at first. Authoring a second book seemed overwhelming. I have two more books I want to write over the next few years, but since writing is my third career, it's a complex task. How do I apply these manifestation tactics toward meeting my writing goals? Following the advice from my coach in 2023, I stopped looking at the finish line and started looking at simply doing each day and actualizing the writing process by committing to one hour each day.

Can you find one hour every day? Most answers are yes, whether first thing in the morning, over a lunch break, or curled up in bed with a laptop instead of reading that book. It could be over your afternoon tea or coffee. Commit and manifest one hour per day. During that one hour, don't allow any interruptions. Commit to sitting still, putting your hands on the keyboard, and simply typing the thoughts for that section without doing any editing.

Chapter 11

This works. There are no big goals, just baby bites that make it easy to hit my mark daily and leave the feelings of procrastination and overwhelming anxiety behind.

To make those small, bite-sized tasks work even more effectively for you, you want to use sales goal manifestation. Let the Phoenix rise and change begin, in the next chapter I'll give you more concrete ideas to change the operative behaviors and begin to buy back time and eliminate on the job stress.

CHAPTER 12

Humanizing Tasks

Time-Management Skills to Maximize Operational Success

Mastering time management isn't just a skill—it's been an integral force in my personal and professional life. Yes, this was a more minor topic in the big picture of *The Art of Selling, We Make Order Makers, Not Order Takers:* however, business owners and entrepreneurs have been screaming for more! So, I'm still talking about it! Every. Single. Day.

Chapter 12

Prioritization

Okay, we did a lot of prioritizations in chapter five. Remember the new perspective we have when looking at our accounts? The same method applies when deciding how we are spending our time day to day, week to week, month to month. This is where you will find the time to buy back! Let me illustrate how to conceptualize prioritizing using familiar business scenarios and how simple it becomes with effective time-management solutions.

As I sit here writing this chapter from my kitchen table, juggling multiple roles in a small business while relying on a contract from another to stay afloat, I genuinely understand the importance of time management and prioritization techniques. I can plan my week meticulously, dedicating Tuesdays to creative work, reserving Wednesdays through Fridays for coaching clients, and setting aside one week each month for my contractual sales agent duties. But, as many of you know, plans don't always unfold as expected.

- ▶ Prioritize sales above all else.
- ▶ Make closing deals your primary focus.
- ▶ Make following up with existing clients and previous conversations a priority over the new shiny entity that just walked through the door.

Everything else should come second. If a lucrative lead pops up, my social media creative time will have to wait. If a client wants to schedule a face-to-face meeting, it must be at their convenience, not mine.

Consider once again the Pareto principle, or the 80/20 rule.

Remember those customers who would spend hours discussing options for their projects? The challenge arises when showroom staff need help to prioritize their time, fearing they might lose a sale if they cut the meeting short. This dynamic perfectly encapsulates the interplay between perception, prioritization, and the Pareto principle.

Prioritizing accounts and outreach

Prioritizing accounts and outreach efforts ensures that we're not just busy, but productive. It means dedicating our time and energy to the opportunities that promise the greatest return. By focusing on key accounts and targeted outreach, we can optimize our efforts and achieve better results with the same or even less work. Why is this so critical? Without a clear prioritization strategy, it's easy to become reactive and respond to whatever demands attention next rather than what is most beneficial for our business goals. This can lead to missed opportunities and inefficiencies, directly impacting our bottom line.

I emphasize the use of visualization tools to assist in this prioritization process. Visualization shows where we should concentrate most of our time expenditures.

For instance, using tools like dashboards or visual mapping techniques, we can quickly identify which accounts drive the most revenue, which prospects hold the highest potential, and where our outreach can yield the best results. At least once every few months, I loved to go into my boss's office and take over the whiteboard, especially when I began training the other associates. It was not only important that I knew what accounts' priorities were but also that my team understood those priorities.

Chapter 12

When I use this with my coaching clients, the best part is watching the light bulb click on as they recognize what activities they employ daily that need to be pushed up to the top of the list and which ones need to fall to the wayside.

So, let's get started, follow the examples by handwriting or making a spreadsheet of all the functions your business performs on an average day and week. Knowing that we don't do the same things on the same day, really consider all the tasks required during the week. Below are a few examples: entrepreneur/solopreneur, (B2C) retail, and (B2B) wholesale salesperson schedule breakdowns.

Showroom (B2C) Example

Business Function/Task	Time Needed to Complete	Ranking (A, B, C)
Email Correspondence/Follow Up	1–2 hours	
Quote Data Entry	One hour	
Appointment Scheduling	30 minutes	
Cold Calling/Lead Development	30 minutes	
Follow-Up Phone Calls	30 minutes	
Entering Data into the CRM	Two hours	
Making Social Media Content	Four hours	
Research & Development—Project	One hour	
Site Visits	Two hours	
Cleaning Showroom	30 minutes	
Outside Sales Visits	Four hours	
Inside Sales Visits/Appointments	Four hours	
Writing Thank-you Notes	30 minutes	

BEYOND ORDER MAKERS

Entrepreneur/Small Business/Coach Example

Business Function/Task	Time Needed to Complete	Ranking (A, B, C)
Accounting	1-2 hours each week	
Social Media Creative	Four hours each week	
Sales	Two hours each day	
Client Appointments (varies) 3 x day	15 hours each week	
Organizing/Cleaning Office	One hour each week	
Email Correspondence	One hour each day	
Outside Selling (varies)	Four hours each week	
Networking	One hour each week	
Volunteer Work	One hour each week	
Other Creative Functions	2-4 hours each week	
Follow-Up	One hour each day	

Account Manager/Wholesale (B2B) Example

Business Function/Task	Time Needed to Complete	Ranking (A, B, C)
Email Correspondence/Follow Up	1-2 hours	
Quote Data Entry	One hour	
Appointment Scheduling	30 minutes	
Cold Calling/Lead Development	30 minutes	
Follow-Up Phone Calls	30 minutes	
Entering Data into the CRM	Two hours	
Making Social Media Content	4-20 hours per week	
Research & Development—Project	1-2 hours each week	
Site Visits	Two hours each week	
Outside Sales Visits	Six hours each day	
Inside Sales Visits/Appointments	Four hours each week	

Chapter 12

Writing Thank-you Notes	30 minutes each week	
Inventory Check & Update Photos	One hour each week	
Offers & Weekly Specials	1–2 hours each week	
Networking	1–2 hours each week	
Calendar Planning	One hour each week	

Before moving on, go back and add any monthly, quarterly or annual tasks too!

> ***Pro Tip!*** *Consider asking another entrepreneur, a coach, or a trusted business associate who knows you well and can help you see things you might overlook.*

Now that we've gotten our tasks written out on paper, it's time to consider the Pareto principle and how we need to rank the importance of each task. Remember, tasks that help you deposit, close deals, or put money in the bank will always be an "A." The subsequent supportive tasks, data entry, and organization will also fall under "B" or "C." Think hard about relevancy to making sales and building leads for sales.

This is where it gets tricky and what I find the most interesting when I ask my clients to create this chart and we review it together. It never fails: our emails always fall on the top of the list. *Why is that?*

According to the Harvard Business Review, France even passed a law making it illegal to answer business correspondence after work hours.[76] Woah! Also, according to Harvard Business Review, "The average worker checks their email 15 times per day—or every 37 minutes. So, if you're checking your email every 37 minutes—and email interruptions steal almost 30 minutes of your attention and focus—you can see how your inbox might hinder your productivity." [77]

While, yes, communication with clients is *top-tier* valuable, answering correspondence is one of those things we can always come back to at any given time during the day or week.

> ***Pro tip**—Set multiple blocks each day and an alarm to check and respond to emails. I recommend spending no less than thirty minutes each session and then going back to the other prioritized tasks.*

Remember back in chapter six when I provided current statistics for emailing? Why wouldn't we consider prioritizing our email schedule with the optimal times to email our clients? You can make the determination of which statistics are accurate for your exact business model, and we can always program our emails to send during specific times, making our work more efficient.

---

[76] Chamorro-Premuzic, Tomas. "Why the French Email Law Won't Restore Work-Life Balance." *Harvard Business Review*, January 2017. https://hbr.org/2017/01/why-the-french-email-law-wont-restore-work-life-balance.

[77] Sonne, Laura Mae Martin. "How to Spend Way Less Time on Email Every Day." *Harvard Business Review*, January 2019. https://hbr.org/2019/01/how-to-spend-way-less-time-on-email-every-day.

Chapter 12

I have an old school mentality about deciding when phone calls take precedence over emails, so remember to take that into consideration while setting priorities. Phone calls often solve problems, answer questions directly, and cut through the red tape faster than emails anyway, so why not consider prioritizing telephone follow-up over email?

By mastering the art of prioritization and utilizing the right visualization tools, you transform your approach to time management from reactive to proactive, from scattered to strategic. You enhance efficiency and amplify your effectiveness, driving you toward your business goals precisely and purposefully.

Put the work to work!

If you've taken the notion to rank tasks around your business to heart, you have a pretty nifty cheat sheet for time blocking and creating more time for yourself. At this point, it's time to move to the calendar and plot the work! Take each of your categories, A, B, and C, and start conceptualizing a single work week or a single work month.

Sometimes, it helps to begin with a monthly view and drop in the tasks that only need a little bit of time monthly. Select days in which you can hold yourself accountable to be in the office and lock in these monthly A, B, or C tasks right away.

Next, drop down into a weekly view and start plotting those A-level tasks. Consider the days of the week that coincide with each task. Using the chart example, I might decide that Tuesdays are the days I will dedicate my four hours to social media content creation. Since I'm using a planner now, I don't need to do this every week (amazing, right?).

Outside sales, I need to get out and visit customers for at least four hours each week. Using my intuition, I know the best day of the week to do this is Wednesday, so I'll go ahead and block that off.

Friday is a great day for follow-up, catching up, setting appointments, and closing out data entry. I won't take any afternoon appointments on Fridays, allotting myself an entire half-day to accomplish these tasks.

A client told me, "I feel like I'm walking in new shoes on Monday mornings". A local designer in Richmond, VA, exclaimed how this process changed her perspective when returning to the office after a weekend break. She no longer scrambled to read and respond to emails. She had a task list prepared from her Friday follow-up hours that gave her direction and comfort after she had rested her mind from the business tasks over the weekend. Ahhh, can you feel the relief?

If you're getting the picture by now, I encourage you to give this scheduling method a try for a month and see how much ease and comfort is created by being more prepared, organized, and overall planning ahead to avoid the squirrel scramble at the beginning of each week.

> **Pro tip**—*Turn off notifications on your phone and employ "Do Not Disturb" functions regularly during times when you need focus.*

Chapter 12

Using a Thirty-Day Calendar

When it comes to time management, I get a lot of laughs when I bring up my old thirty-day calendar routine. I don't know why people make fun of me for using this tool because it really works. So laugh all you'd like, as I describe how this little tool works wonders.

My first thirty-day calendar experience

I felt like living a dream when I got a remote job. No more rushing to the retail shop before it opened. No more commuting to Ralph Lauren on the New York subway system. Now, I had the freedom to manage my schedule, just like so many remote workers in the post Covid society. But there was one problem: I didn't know where to start. My employer gave me an internal account system, but I was the first rep ever in this territory, so there weren't any accounts to hack! With very little data. I had to chart a path for business development (sales) by finding and making in-person visits to local and regional kitchen and bath remodeling firms, cabinet companies, interior design firms, and businesses willing to display the collection of countertop surfaces I was hired to promote.

It was overwhelming, I used search engines and began making a few lists, but I was green, very green, and it was hard to grasp how I would visit all these cities and people on a repetitive basis. So, one day I went to an office supply store and purchased a large thirty-day calendar. Organizing the accounts by city, I began to plot my days over the course of a month. Adding in my office hours, before I knew it, I had a travel plan! My very first ever **mind map for business development**. I had no idea how far this little tool would take me.

BEYOND ORDER MAKERS

The thirty-day calendar helped me visualize a month of days at once. I also

- got a weekly planner to write who I would visit each day of the week
- used a mapping program to find more leads
- prioritized Mondays and Fridays close to home for office time
- made distinct repetitive travel plans for Tuesdays, Wednesdays, and Thursdays monthly
- accounted for faraway cities that needed less attention
- discovered smaller cities to include during overnight trips

This visualization and first effort at time blocking helped me develop a natural instinct for when I needed to visit clients. After a year, I no longer needed that thirty-day calendar, as I had developed an instinct to prioritize top areas and include lower priorities on a less frequent basis.

253

Chapter 12

The little weekly planner paid off too! Initially, I would note down six or seven accounts per day based on my monthly outline. I continued doing this for several years before switching to the digital version of the weekly planner, my CRM. Funnily enough, I started memorizing key accounts in each city after the first year. I could always cross-check with my CRM, but soon, I didn't need to rely on it. I could just use my eyes to drive around each location, and sometimes, I would come across new opportunities. To further drive home this very basic and useful step, another story.

Case Study: A new perspective on travel

One of my networking groups (WIFI) has a bi-annual mentorship program. I was recruited to jump in during the summer cohort to mentor an amazing and experienced commercial sales representative, April. Our mentorship started off casual and while flooring was a little foreign to me, I knew we were brought together for a reason and before long, April began describing how uneventful and unorganized her travel felt working her very large territory of South Dakota.

April has tons of experience, but through our discussions and having her use my chapter five approach of target marketing, we were able to then apply this thirty-day calendar technique and incorporate new vigor into her planning.

Once again, watching the lightbulb clink over to bright mode, makes for a success story. April has recorded a testimonial you can see online about how this little tool gave her a new perspective on organizing travel, while allowing her flexibility to construct her work around her personal life (kids). This refreshed approach brought her peace and comfort knowing the next thirty, sixty, ninety days have plans that don't conflict with her children's needs, and she also has a new client list to approach based on research we found in chapter five.

So, if you don't think this method is for you, give it a chance. Try taking a visual approach to your time management and before long, intuition will commence.

Time Blocking and Sales

Time blocking is one of the most effective strategies in my work, and we spend a great deal of time perfecting it during my sales training efforts. **Time blocking** allows for specific time slots for different sales activities, such as prospecting, client meetings, creativity, quoting, and follow-up. By setting aside and forecasting how we will spend our day, we ensure all critical tasks receive dedicated attention. We literally create space to complete the necessary tasks.

Time blocking is about creating a structure that allows us to control the dynamic of day-to-day activities. When I collaborate with clients on this topic, I often hear them feeling overwhelmed:

- "I run out of time during the day meeting clients in the showroom; there is no time left for follow-up."
- "I can't find time to make my social media posts advertising our services."
- "We deal with walk-in traffic, so there is no way to stop traffic flow."
- "I get lost in the day when I'm outside traveling, and before I know it, I'm getting home at 6–7 p.m. and exhausted, so I forget to enter my data into the CRM."
- "I've zero time to work on my social media presence."

I promise we can regain control and feel less overwhelmed with the right time-management strategies.

Moving forward into how **time blocking** can affect sales goals, we can attack this conversation in two ways: how you control the dynamic in the office and how you utilize data to make your selling more effective and increase sales.

When most people consider time blocking, they think about hours during the week. Besides sales training and coaching, I am still a salesperson! I conduct business development and lead generation for Grassi Pietre SRL. Staying in tune with construction materials helps keep me in tune with the topics I teach, and it helps me stay connected with the stone industry from my roots. I have to time-block everything! I don't believe there are enough exclamation points to put behind time-blocking when it comes to managing two companies, volunteering in several women's organizations, marketing creative, writing books, staying sober, and having a fur family. **Never enough time; find your path to managing it! No week will ever be the same, but we can set goals!**

To relay the message further, let's look at a recent coaching client.

Case Study: Getting out of the office challenge

My client struggled with literally getting out of the office. In her case, sales don't happen unless we are seeing clients face to face. I asked her to set specific office days to meet clients and identify out-of-office hours to chase new clients and approach them directly in their elements (proactive selling). This client has trouble with setting and keeping this schedule each week. The winning solution for her team and work requirements is to create the schedule for the following week on Friday afternoons. The priority on Fridays is to set aside time to look at accounts, quotes, prospects, sample deliveries, and events. She had to force herself to block out two hours and commit to shutting down the phone and focusing on pulling CRM data, reviewing the week she is closing, and applying the tasks in a structured format for the following Monday through Friday.

The key to successful time blocking is setting and following our own rules. My client had these "self-regulating rules":

- On Mondays, we have sales meetings.
- I need to be home early on Wednesdays because of Church.
- On Fridays, I must set up the in-office vs out-of-office timing for the following week.
- Next Thursday evening, I need to attend an event in XXXX.
- Every other month, I must travel three hours to see a client in Dallas.

Based on her needs, I advised my client to block off specific days every week to prioritize her personal and professional needs. In her case, she should identify two days to be "out" to meet clients and ensure consistency in the showroom. All errands, outside sales calls, sample board requests, and monetary collections should be scheduled on these two days. Grouping these together helped structure and relieve my client's schedule while balancing her personal and professional commitments.

Hey, Technology, Meet Time Management!

Grab a pen and paper, and let's explore some tools that have helped me tremendously become organized and free up time for more important activities, like having fun with my fur babies.

Cloud computing and storage

The flexibility and accessibility offered by cloud software are unparalleled. Popular platforms such as Google Drive, Dropbox, and Microsoft OneDrive offer the convenience of seamless sharing and collaboration on various documents and projects. This ensures that teams can work together efficiently, no matter where they are physically situated. While most professionals are on board with using these programs, especially established larger companies, my private small business clients still struggle to get on board. Scrolling the internet, I find that even large organizations are starting to move away from corporate cloud systems and integrate back to internal servers; however, for the average mom-and-pop business, we are tied to the major companies providing large storage capacities. My absolute best reason for getting started as soon as possible with all storage on shared platforms: mobility. As an entrepreneur or small business or even salesperson for a small business, we must move around. The office isn't always where we work, and we need the flexibility to pull data from all devices.

Project management tools

Utilizing project management tools such as Asana, Trello, or Monday helps us track progress, assign tasks, and meet deadlines. These tools visually represent project timelines and individual responsibilities, fostering accountability and clarity. In my industry, PM tools are necessary, and they need to integrate with my other systems to enhance communication. Some project management software includes CRM systems! A double win!

Trello, for instance, is a team interface that allows users to split up tasks, assign leaders and priorities, and create boards for specific projects. When expanding my website to include funnel systems, I hired a subcontractor, and Trello worked wonders, allowing us to communicate on our opposite time schedules since she lived in the Philippines. We can each work individually on specific segments and alert the other player if necessary. As we complete tasks, we communicate via text, links to documents, and visuals created by request. Slack works similarly.

Monday integrates with my local fabricators' cutting technologies and is a favorite within my stone and surface industry.

Zoho, a software company with social media scheduling tools and CRM capabilities, is a multifaceted powerhouse; however, the social tools were too limited for my needs.

ClickUp is another small business software like Trello! This one incorporates timesheets, finance, human resource tools, and operational tools. Remember that automation is transforming daily, and various PM tools will include intelligence-based automation architecture to transform what we must recall and recite, virtually eliminating the human responsibilities of following up and capturing sales data. Automation tools like Zapier and IFTTT can streamline repetitive tasks by connecting different apps and services. For instance, automating email responses or data entry processes can save time and reduce the risk of errors. Simple yet powerful tools like Todoist, Microsoft To

Do, and Wunderlist can help individuals and teams manage their daily tasks.

I'm listing a handful of companies and their significance based on personal perspectives. Regardless of the type of small business we are running, I hope you will find the appropriate tool for staying organized and maintaining smooth communication with subcontractors or employees.

Integrated communication systems

Messaging, video calls, and file sharing are seamlessly integrated into Slack, Microsoft Teams, and Zoom platforms. By centralizing communication, these systems reduce the likelihood of missing vital information and improve team coordination. The service known as GoTo Meeting is used by one of the industry groups I am associated with, but there is a noticeable shift toward Microsoft Teams because of its extensive integrations on a global scale. I would also include Trello in this conversation, based on my personal usage. Trello allows me to operate with subs in other countries and communicate tasks effectively.

Data analytics and reporting

Do you own a website? You need data analytic software! Even if I never sold a book or product online, I love reading data analytics to help me improve the website and items I want customers to see first. Data analytics tools like Google Analytics, Tableau, and Power BI can offer businesses valuable insights into their performance, enabling them to make informed decisions. I find Semrush to be a preferable option over Google Analytics.

Additionally, considering the limited availability in my schedule, I would rather rely on someone with a deeper understanding of these tools to manage and monitor them, as it would be challenging for me to properly supervise them. Given that I am running a small business, I need to keep track of the website traffic and the outcomes of my marketing emails. However, I can delegate the integration of SEO strategies and make necessary enhancements to my website to a subcontractor.

> **Pro tip**—SEO (search engine optimization) and SEM (search engine marketing) are the entrepreneurs best friends: Well-implemented SEO and SEM strategies ensure that our business is front and center during the awareness and consideration stage, capturing attention of our buyers.

While it is probably better suited to professionals, it is equally essential for business owners or salespeople to possess a certain level of knowledge to understand the operations of tools and the interpretation of data. Although I rely on others to handle the "tweaking" aspect, I have invested time and effort into acquiring the skills to interpret and understand the data. Thanks to this newfound ability, I can now make more strategic decisions regarding business and visual identity changes. With the help of these tools, I can enhance my ability to make data-driven decisions, as they assist me in identifying trends and assessing the effectiveness of various strategies.

Chapter 12

Digital note-taking

One of the coolest current trends involves AI for note-taking! Once the iPad generation began, companies developed ways we could transcribe our notes with apps like Evernote, OneNote, and Notion, allowing for organized and easily searchable notes. Have you been on a Zoom call where someone is employing Otter.ai? It is literally the coolest thing to take notes while the conference call is going along, and no one has to take notes! Otter.ai transcribes the entire meeting into a document ready to save in a client's file.

I'm just getting used to OneNote because I'm so pre-programmed to use notebooks day by day. Rolling over to digital note-taking is new and difficult for me personally, but it is the wave of the future. The other day, I was in a volunteer group meeting. One of my coworkers had a "Kindle" device designed completely for digital note translation and organization called "reMarkable." It is easier to use than OneNote but is currently priced at $500. OneNote is the least expensive option since I already have Microsoft across all my devices. Hopefully, similar devices will come to market soon, and the value of economics will drive the price down to a more economical investment.

If you give instructions and create "process" documents, there's an app for that! (Pun intended.) You don't need someone from IT or HR to make a Word document with pictures and arrows pointing out various nodes of instructions. Instead, use Scribe. Now, making visual instruction documents can happen in minutes, not hours. It allows users to capture workflows and document procedures with ease. Scribe automatically generates visual, easy-to-follow instructions, which can be invaluable for training new employees, maintaining consistency in processes, and ensuring critical tasks are executed correctly. I'm seriously impressed!

By integrating technological solutions into our practices, we can automate repetitive tasks, saving valuable time and allowing employees to focus on more meaningful work. For example, implementing project management software can help streamline task allocation, collaboration, and progress tracking, ensuring that projects are completed efficiently and on time. Additionally, using cloud storage solutions eliminates the need for physical paperwork, reduces clutter, and makes information easily accessible from anywhere.

Moreover, leveraging technology allows for effective management of personal and professional tasks. Digital calendars, task management applications, and communication tools enable individuals to prioritize and schedule their activities, ensuring they stay on top of deadlines and responsibilities.

Integrating technological solutions into our practices supports a productive and efficient work environment, fostering growth and success. I hope you find some suggestions in this chapter helpful. At the very least, I've sparked a few ideas about making an investment decision to assist with time management and organization. While I understand this can be overwhelming, I'm here to help! Make a list of your challenges and write to me if I can help you brainstorm one of these programs to suit your needs.

Chapter 12

Follow-Up

One of my most popular topics is follow-up, a transformative closing element that most salespeople should spend more time refining. As an entrepreneur or business owner, it's tough out there! It's tough to find time, people, and customers and remember to follow up.

But we can't forget the follow-up. This is the most required skill, period, for anyone wanting to sell anything: the art of follow-up.

Follow-up is the glue that holds the sales process together. It's not just about customer service; it's not simply about reminding a potential customer of an offer; it's about reinforcing our commitment and building a relationship based on trust and reliability. Follow-up is essential.

(make into a checklist)

- Consistent follow-up shows that we are dependable and committed to addressing the customer's needs, building a foundation of trust.
- Regular contact ensures that our product or service remains at the forefront of the customer's mind when they are ready to make a purchase decision.
- Effective follow-up can be the final push that converts a hesitant lead into a confirmed sale.
- Follow-up interactions provide an opportunity to gather valuable feedback, which can be used to improve our products, services, and sales techniques.
- By simply checking in and providing additional information or support, we enhance the customer experience, leading to repeat business and referrals.

RevBoss, a new and up-and-coming outbound sales agency, says, "Customer awareness is at an all-time high, customers can easily see through flimsy techniques . . . "[78]

Given that it is so important, you will want to use the strategies and techniques covered in this chapter.

Empathy and Emotional Intelligence for Follow-Up

We must return to empathy and emotional intelligence (EI) to personalize our follow-up for maximum effectiveness.

Empathy is the ability to be empathetic to others. In follow-up, this means putting yourself in the customer's shoes and considering their needs, concerns, and emotions. Following up with empathy shows your customers that you genuinely care about their experience and satisfaction.

EI, on the other hand, is the ability to recognize, understand, and manage one's own and others' emotions. High EI allows one to navigate social complexities, foster strong relationships, and make informed decisions. In follow-up, EI helps one respond appropriately to customer emotions, whether they are happy, frustrated, or indifferent.

Incorporate empathy and EI into your follow-up practices:

Listen actively. When *you* follow up, listen to customers' feedback, acknowledge *their* concerns, and address issues, you demonstrate how *their* input indicates improvement in *their* experience.

---

[78] RevBoss. "5 Sales Follow-Up Techniques You Should Be Using Every Day." Last modified [July 2024]. https://revboss.com/blog/5-sales-follow-up-techniques-you-should-be-using-every-day.

Personalize your approach. Tailor your follow-up communications to each customer. Reference previous interactions, acknowledge their specific needs, and offer relevant solutions. This personalized approach shows that you see them as individuals, not just another sale.

Be genuine. Authenticity is key to building trust. Avoid using scripted responses, and instead, speak from the heart. Customers can sense when you are being genuine, which helps strengthen your relationship.

Respond promptly. Timely follow-up shows that you respect your customers' time and are attentive to their needs. Even if you don't have an immediate solution, letting them know you are working on it and will get back to them soon can go a long way to maintaining their trust.

Show appreciation. Acknowledge your customers' business and express gratitude for their feedback, whether it's positive or negative. Showing appreciation helps to build a positive rapport and encourages ongoing engagement.

Manage your emotions. Stay calm and composed, especially when dealing with demanding customers or situations. High EI means not letting our emotions interfere with our professional interactions. Instead, focus on resolving issues and providing a positive experience for the customer.

Clearly define the next steps. Summarize the conversation! Tell them exactly what needs to happen next, making this process easy.

> **Pro Tip**—*Prepare the next steps in advance so you aren't caught on the spot. Visualize the outcome and be prepared to lay out exactly how we want the client to follow through.*

During the active conversation, take the time to set the tone for the next steps: how you will be in touch and when.

Using Technology in the Follow-Up

Technology can boost follow-up. The tech tips below are based on services that make my human capabilities more powerful for effective follow-up:

CRM systems. CRM systems are the backbone of effective follow-up strategies. They help organize customer data, track interactions, and set reminders for future follow-ups. By keeping all customer information in one place, salespeople can access a comprehensive view of each client's history and preferences, allowing for more personalized and relevant follow-ups.

Automated email campaigns. Email automation tools can schedule and send personalized follow-up emails based on customer actions or timelines. For instance, if a potential client downloads a brochure from your website, an automated email can follow up with additional information or a meeting request. Automation ensures that no follow-up opportunity is missed and that customers receive timely communications.

What about scheduling email follow-ups on the calendar? This little tip will save your life!

Most email systems have follow-up capabilities, regardless of the system. (Outlook, MailChimp, Gmail, Mail, and Yahoo, etc.) Whatever the system chosen for business emails, look in the help section if you cannot locate the follow-up features. I'll include one of my favorite follow-up techniques using Outlook's "flag" and "pin" systems. Flagging an email allows me to pay attention to this message until I choose to file it away. I can ask the system for quick reminders by using the follow-up feature option. Outlook allows us to flag individual emails, and we have an option to select follow-up *tomorrow*, *this week*, *next week*, or *no date* for alerts; however, even better is my personal follow-up system using Outlook's drag-and-drop system. (Admittedly, this was easier in the "old Outlook.")

Have you tried opening the little calendar icon with a check mark in Outlook? Have you ever tried dragging an item from your inbox over to this icon? **Dragging and dropping communication into my calendar** allows me to pull any string of communication from my Inbox or Sent mail and drag it over the calendar icon on the left. Once I drop the email into the calendar, an event scheduler pops up, and I can choose the date and time and add any details I need to the event. I also have the option to create a meeting out of this email! Since the email has a subject, that automatically becomes the event topic and includes anyone in the email chain as invitees! It's magic! This trick can also be tweaked to a simple reminder by removing the people from the event, it becomes a dated event set for me to be reminded to follow-up. This is a game-changer—try it! Instead of depending on the limited flags for follow-up, I can now set the event on my calendar and notifications so I will not miss the specific day and time I need to reach this person.

> **Pro Tip** – Try scheduling all follow-up as an event on your calendar! If in a conversation and someone alerts you to a specific time, they want you to follow up, go ahead and add it your phone immediately.

Video messaging or video calling. Video messages and the use of video calls add a distinctive touch to follow-ups. Tools like Loom or Vidyard allow salespeople to record personalized video messages for their clients. Most cellphones are equipped with video calling features, and many use apps to accomplish this. Free apps like Facebook Messenger call feature, WhatsApp (owned by Facebook) are used globally. A video follow-up can make an impression and demonstrate a higher level of commitment and personalization compared to text-based communications.

Scheduling tools. Tools like Calendly or Doodle simplify scheduling follow-up meetings. These tools integrate with your calendar and allow clients to book available time slots, eliminating the back and forth of finding a mutually convenient time. This efficiency can significantly enhance the follow-up process and improve client satisfaction.

A quick story from one of my clients: Gail mentioned she keeps losing clients in her showroom because she's busy with another client. Walk-in traffic arrives while she is obligated to another customer, and even though she says hello and mentions she will be with them momentarily, often they leave the store without further interaction. How can she capture all those moments and create a follow-up on the spot?

Prepare for scheduling an appointment on the spot, have an iPad or phone or computer tool readily available so the client can quickly enter follow-up information and have the option to schedule their own personalized appointment with you. Presenting that data capturing tool instead of saying "I'll be right with you" can make or break whether we have repeat and satisfactory interactions even while obligated to other clients.

Creating an Effective Follow-Up Action Plan

- **Identify your goals:** Determine whether your follow-up efforts are intended to increase customer satisfaction, boost repeat sales, or gather valuable feedback. Clearly defining your objectives is essential.
- **Segment your customer base:** Tailor your follow-up approaches to different customer segments. New customers may require more educational content about your products while returning customers might appreciate personalized offers or loyalty rewards.
- **Establish a timeline:** Define appropriate times to reach out after initial contact, a sale, or a service interaction. Customize this timeline to fit your industry and meet customer expectations.
- **Select and implement tools such as CRM systems within a timely manner:** "Rome wasn't built in a day," but we need to employ email marketing platforms and task management tools to streamline our follow-up process and ensure no customer is overlooked. Establishing a time "limit" to accomplish the incorporation of technology will help keep everyone on task.
- **Train your team:** Provide comprehensive training sessions that cover the importance of follow-up, effective

communication techniques, and how to use the tools implemented. Conduct role-playing scenarios and schedule regular practice rounds to help your team refine their skills. The very last section of this book has tips on where and how to find training to assist.

▸ **Foster a positive mindset:** Encourage your team to view follow-up as an opportunity rather than a chore. Share success stories and regularly review and provide feedback on follow-up performance to keep your team engaged.

▸ **Regular evaluation and adjustment:** Continuously evaluate and adjust your follow-up strategy based on feedback from your team and customers. Stay adaptable and be willing to refine your approach to meet your business goals and customer needs.

Follow-up Fun

I employed AI to help me come up with some games we could play with friends or sales staff to teach the art of follow-up. I hope you get a chance to incorporate these ideas for a sales team if that is your role, or as an entrepreneur, you can try them on your own and see what ideas come forth.

Chapter 12

Follow-Up Bingo

Setup.

Create bingo cards with different follow-up actions and scenarios in each square.

Examples include

- Follow up with a client after a meeting
- Send a personalized thank-you note
- Respond to a client inquiry within 24 hours
- Schedule a follow-up call
- Offer additional product information

How to play.

- Each salesperson gets a bingo card at the beginning of the week.
- As they complete each follow-up task, they mark off the corresponding square.
- The first person to complete a row, column, or diagonal shouts, "Bingo!" and wins a small prize.

"Decision Tree" Follow-Up Game

Setup.

Prepare a set of cards with different follow-up scenarios, such as:

- Client hasn't responded to your initial proposal
- Client expressed interest but hasn't made a decision
- Client needs more information about a product
- Client is unhappy with a recent purchase

How to play.

- Pair up salespeople and have them take turns drawing a scenario card.
- One person plays the salesperson, and the other plays the client.
- The salesperson must practice their follow-up skills based on the scenario while the client provides feedback on their approach.
- Rotate roles and scenarios to give everyone a chance to practice different situations.

Chapter 12

Follow-Up "Race"

Setup.

Create a list of follow-up tasks that need to be completed, such as sending thank-you emails, scheduling follow-up calls, or providing additional resources to clients.

How to play.

- Set a time limit and have sales team members race to complete the tasks on the list.
- The first person or team to complete all the tasks wins a prize or recognition.
- (Remember, these tasks should be spread out over several days or a week, with regular check-in meetings to ensure the team stays on track.)

CHAPTER 13

Manifestation Selling

A New Perspective on Setting and Achieving Sales Goals

Il gran finale. Get ready for the Grand Finale. I get excited when I help people meet and exceed their sales goals. It brings me great satisfaction to watch my clients win! I also love teaching killer mindset techniques. As we embark on the final leg of this crazy Rep Methods journey, pack your bags and let's have some more fun!

Chapter 13

In this chapter I'll teach you how to build that infallible pipeline I mentioned early on through what I like to call **manifestation selling**.

Manifestation History

Oxford Languages defines manifestation as "the action or fact of showing an abstract idea" and "an event, action, or object that clearly shows or embodies something, especially a theory or an abstract idea."[79]

In Dr. Tara Burton's essay "The Long, Strange History of 'Manifesting,'" she explains more about the history of this somewhat strange topic. "Beyond the 21st century and back to the 19th, to a little-known but once extraordinarily popular American religious tradition known as New Thought, or the 'mind cure.'"[80]

The concept of manifesting sales as a strategy remains largely unexplored in sales literature, despite its ancient core principles. Manifestation topics gained traction during the pandemic, riding the wave of increased interest in online spiritualism and self-help. This concept is prevalent in Reddit articles, YouTube videos, and blog posts, yet it still needs to be explored in traditional *sales* literature. Finding supportive research on this topic has been a challenge. In the end, these are still personal and unproven, and some might even call the

---

[79] Oxford Languages. "Manifestation." Oxford English Dictionary. Accessed August 20, 2024.
https://www.google.com/search?q=manifestation&rlz=1C1CHBF_enUS895US895&oq=manifestation.

[80] Burton, Tara Isabella. "The Long, Strange History of 'Manifesting.'" *The New York Times*. Accessed March 9, 2024.
https://www.nytimes.com/2024/03/09/opinion/manifesting-spirituality-america-reality.html

process a bit "woo-woo". Take it for what it's worth, I've found proof in using these techniques.

Tony Robbins writes, "When you are truly able to visualize your goals, you'll be happy within yourself."[81] Isn't happiness what we are truly after? Doesn't meeting or exceeding our goals bring us joy? Sanjana Gupta writes for Verywell Mind[82], a popular blog about mental health and wellness. Before we get to my magic number technique, here are some amazing manifestation techniques presented by Gupta that people are already using every day.

Law of attraction

The law of attraction "states that what we focus on is what we will attract in life"[83]. There are several printed books about this subject and even more blogs, videos, and social media posts formulated around this quite simple topic. By keeping what we want in front of our minds, we will manifest it into a reality.

Create a vision board

We did this in college before creating visual merchandising plans or executing a business plan. Interior designers use this method before presenting to a client their vision for the space. They have the option of collecting photos, tangible fabrics, items from our sheds, whatever they need to create a vision of

---

[81] Robbins, Tony. "How to Focus: Goal Visualization." *Tony Robbins.* Accessed Aug 20, 2024. https://tonyrobbins.com/how-to-focus/goal-visualization.

[82] ¹ Gupta, S. (n.d.) *Manifestation Techniques: Harnessing the Power of Your Mind*, Verywell Mind. Available at: https://www.verywellmind.com/manifestation-techniques (Accessed: 28 October 2024).

[83] "The Law of Attraction: What We Focus on Is What We Attract," *Psychology Today*, accessed October 29, 2024, https://www.psychologytoday.com.

the task they want to accomplish. Putting together a vision board is an ideal way to look at what you want for the future and visualize it, accept it, and ideally achieve it.

Create Visual Goals Board

Grab a dry erase board, or cork board and hang it somewhere visible to you every day while you are working. Add items to this board which help you visualize a goal. Try to think big and try to capitalize on dreams you have. Choose pictures or objects that help you visualize meeting this goal. Such as writing a check to yourself for the payday of your dreams? Maybe it's a home you plan to buy one day by a waterway or beach. Maybe it's a place you intend to visit. For example, have you heard about Jim Carrey, the actor from the 1990s? Early in his career Mr. Carrey wrote out a check for $10 million dollars to himself and inscribed in the memo: "acting services rendered." He dated the check for 1995. Just before Thanksgiving 1995, he found out he was going to make $10 million on *Dumb and Dumber.*"[84] The check he wrote to himself was still in his wallet!

3-6-9 method

According to Gupta, write down your goals: three times in the morning, six times in the afternoon, nine times in the evening. Although she doesn't specify for how long we do this, I found blog claims that one or two weeks should do the trick.

---

[84] Carrey, Jim. "Jim Carrey Wrote Himself a $10 Million Cheque." *Far Out Magazine*. Accessed August 20, 2024. https://faroutmagazine.co.uk/jim-carrey-wrote-himself-10-million-cheque/.

Gupta talks a lot about getting out of our comfort zone, staying clear on what we want, visualizing our goals, keeping statements and actions positive, and articulating goals.

Similarly, Alcoholics Anonymous claims that if I'm angry at a person, I can repeat the sick man's prayer repeatedly and that will help me release the grudge in a relatively short amount of time.[85]

Manifestation in Sales

Applying this technique to my sales training, I want to examine the impact of positivity and manifestation, infusing each day with wins. Daily victories make it more appealing to go to work every day, don't you think? Winning keeps me from burning out.

I can't wait to tell you more because it's the perfect chance for newcomers in sales or entrepreneurship to start winning!

My goal manifestation began during one of my *boots on the ground* jobs where sales data and actual sales totals were hidden from me! Yes, the bosses kept productivity data relatively hidden, which was so weird! Why would you hide COGS, margin, and sales totals from the salesperson? Well, I'll tell you, it's usually because a company has something to hide. With the data being withheld for so many years, I needed to find other ways to hold myself accountable for sales goals. Managers would throw numbers at us on conference calls like, "We need the team to sell 14 million dollars annual of X product". It left me wondering how I, as an individual, could meet that goal without knowing what one piece of product cost

---

[85] *Alcoholics Anonymous: The Story of How Many Thousands of Men and Women Have Recovered from Alcoholism.* 4th ed. New York: Alcoholics Anonymous World Services, Inc., 2001.

to make or what were our profit margins when I sold something.

Keeping in mind, most salespeople are financially motivated, we like knowing exactly how commissions end up in our paychecks. In fact, that is the driving force behind experienced salespeople. We know exactly what it takes to produce a certain income, and we learn exactly how to break down the big numbers into a daily, weekly or monthly target. We build our clientele, and we work on building out a pipeline and that's where *the snowball* comes into play.

Building the snowball

Snowballs are created by compacting fresh snow that has a good amount of water content, making them perfect for throwing. Heavy snow is a rare sight in the mid-Atlantic, but when it happens, it's a perfect excuse for everyone to enjoy the outdoors. Imagine starting with a tiny snow pebble and then slowly adding more snow to form a larger snowball. As you roll the snowball along the ground to create a snow person, it gradually increases in size by picking up more snow, just like the gradual growth of a business. As we hit the ground running, we gather clients and sales. We grow and build our pipeline of sales like a snowball rolling down a hill. Also, as we may lose deals or shift into a different path, we might lose some of that snow as it melts away. Amazing correlation don't you think?

Manifestation isn't about the short game, it's for those of us who are in this thing for the long haul.

When it comes to selling, seasoned and accomplished salespeople and business owners tend to focus on long-term goals. As we work, we engage with people, present our ideas, promote the brand, and then later we follow-up, adapting our pitch along the way, understanding the process of closing a deal requires patience. We understand that not all sales can be finalized in a single day, which is often not feasible, especially in my industry. By breaking down significant sales numbers into smaller, achievable targets we can build out an infallible pipeline to meet long-term sales goals. I call this *building the snowball*.

We must start building that *snowball* slowly, adding layer after layer which will build and grow (and melt) along the way.

I want the snowball to keep growing so I can keep the fluid pipeline of sales forming in the background while our space/time continuum and outside influences (I can't control) complete their part of the project.

Both telemarketing companies and retail stores, where I have worked in the past, follow a similar daily sales goal breakdown. They focus on sales associates achieving daily sales objectives, rather than looking at monthly, quarterly, or annual figures.

When I worked for a small personal shopping boutique, slow traffic frustrated the small business owner, leading her to hound us into making telephone calls inciting customers to the store. Frantically we would often play rock, paper, scissors to decide who's turn it was to man the phones. But, in hindsight, what would have happened if our manager proposed breaking down the goal into clothing categories? For example, calling customers for items like cashmere, jeans, or coats based on past purchases. By assigning each salesperson to a specific customer group based on past purchases, we could have

Chapter 13

utilized our POS system more effectively for targeted phone calls. Instead of just inviting customers to the store, our offers and incentives could have been more customized. Isn't hindsight always 20/20?

Real estate professionals have embraced the principles of *The Secret*, a popular book and film about the law of attraction and manifestation. For instance, real estate agents have reported increased success by visualizing their goals and focusing on positive outcomes. In the book, *The Secret*, a fictional character, Sherry, uses manifestation techniques to envision closing high-value deals, which led to a substantial increase in her sales performance and client acquisition.[86]

I want you to also keep in mind how **positive thinking** and **visualization** go hand in hand, helping to create a clear path to achieving goals. We all know positivity is greatly influenced by the implementation of mindfulness techniques, well, so can our sales goals! I assist sales professionals in cultivating resilience and optimism by encouraging them to celebrate small victories, which in turn helps them maintain a positive outlook and face challenges with confidence.

Fueled by this optimism, we stay inspired and motivated to continue pushing for ambitious goals. Confidence is key in successful selling as it empowers us to show trustworthiness and credibility to potential clients.

---

[86] Byrne, Rhonda. *The Secret*. Melbourne: The Secret Publishing, 2006.

Pick a magic number

You know what's fun about breaking down goals into bite sized pieces, selecting a single digit number that becomes a relative and positive affirmation goal for all your tasks. I know, I'm getting a little woo-woo...but stay with me!

Select a single or double-digit number based on some basic tasks you do each day and feels like a workable, achievable goal. Here are some examples:

- Total number of closed sales
- Sales calls in a day
- Lead outreach
- New client development and research time
- Follow-up calls
- Follow-up emails
- Closing a quote and moving into purchase order
- Deposits on future orders
- Words to write
- Product to make
- Sales calls (phone or in person)

Think of this *number* as a winnable item. Don't make it something you can't do! We want to look at this number as something we can accomplish. Remember, we can always adjust later.

Consider a wholesale sales representative tasked with achieving an average monthly revenue of $250,000. $3 million in gross sales, resulting in $1.5 million in net sales after accounting for the cost of goods at a 50 percent keystone markup. To reach the set target, they need to assess the average sale in each transaction and establish a projected value for each sale. In this case, the average transaction is between $5,000 and $10,000, giving a manifestation number of five for a four-week month. **Check out this visual:**

Let's approach this goal from another perspective: Consider a monthly sales goal of $40,000. You may wonder about the simplicity of the math involved. However, the practical application of these figures makes the outcome possible.

Leveraging the number five, the wholesale account manager can employ various strategies, such as making five client calls (apart from in-person visits), visiting five customers daily, closing five sales daily, sending a minimum of five outgoing offers per week, and identifying five new quote opportunities per day. This creativity in application helps to make the seemingly ambitious goal achievable.

Let's examine the potential outcomes that can arise from consistently following these guidelines daily, weekly, and monthly.

Our account manager contacts five customers daily outside of visiting clients. What are they achieving? They are engaging in outreach, setting up future visits, networking, keeping client relationships, informing clients about new inventory or upcoming promotional events, and scheduling appointments for future in-person visits.

They aim to visit five clients in person each day. Although this may not be workable every day of the week, it's still a goal. To get it done, they just need to plan a route for five customers, regardless of the product or service sold. During these in-person visits, the salesperson will inspect inventory and create sales opportunities by following my five steps to selling.

Closing five sales daily is challenging, but it's about accountability. In this case, the target is five sales per week. Setting this goal relieves the pressure of achieving a specific dollar amount. The only thing that matters is that the salesperson reaches five. They could make five transactions of $100 each or five transactions of $2,500 each. The focus should be on holding themselves accountable for quantitative measures rather than solely focusing on total sales dollars. These transactions accumulate over the week and month, culminating in favorable scenarios.

Let's assume that our salesperson abides by the protocol and makes at least five sales per day, each totaling $5,000. Along the way, they sold more than five on some days and on some days they didn't sell anything. On average, this salesperson would achieve nearly $400,000 in monthly gross sales by hitting that daily figure of five. By simplifying goals into singular targets, we can empower our salespeople to do and achieve more, ultimately reaching a higher potential than if a total gross sales goal constrained them as a number.

Here is another example of a smaller monthly total goal broken down into options:

In this sales technique, the number eight is used as a guideline for B2C salespeople.

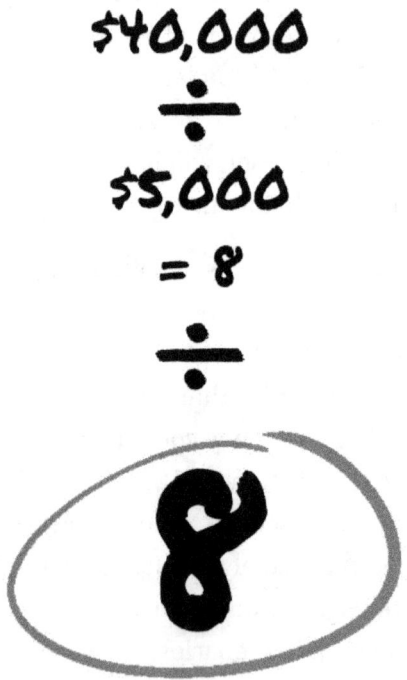

- Eight sales per week.
- Eight follow-up calls per day with post-sales or existing quotes.
- Eight in-store weekly visits with clients by appointment or other means.
- Eight PKs per month with builders, designers, or other accounts.
- Eight events per year for the showroom to invite customers to share experiences inside the showroom/store.

Seems like the number eight is prevalent, and they can apply this as their manifestation sales number.

Create a space for this "magic number" to be seen daily.

I can stay motivated by creating a clear and detailed mental image of hitting this number. This involves visualizing the desired outcome as if it has already been completed, including specific details such as closing a deal, exceeding sales targets, or receiving positive client feedback. By immersing myself in this mental image, I can instill confidence and motivation to act toward realizing those goals.

Practice hitting this number daily.

Implementing a systematic approach to achieving my **magic number** requires consistent effort and dedication. I begin each day with a clear plan outlining specific actions aimed at reaching my daily targets across all designated areas: business development research and outreach, follow-up, closed deals, deposits on future orders, and sales calls. I regularly review and adjust my strategies to optimize performance, ensuring that each activity contributes directly to meeting or exceeding my established goals.

Focusing on daily and weekly milestones allows me to track progress and maintain momentum toward achieving success. Then my daily visualization routines reinforce the practice, maximizing its benefits. By dedicating time each day to visualize success, I maintain focus, motivation, and clarity of purpose. Additionally, it's helpful to incorporate affirmations and positive self-talk into visualization sessions to further reinforce a mindset of success and abundance.

Review with someone else bi-monthly.

Accountability is critical to sustained growth and improvement. Bi-monthly reviews with a trusted partner, whether a teammate, manager, or close business associate, provide an opportunity to assess your performance objectively. Discussing achievements, challenges, and areas for improvement openly can offer valuable insights and perspectives that can lead to strategic adjustments and goal refinements.

Conclusion

As I wrap up this potentially "woo-woo" chapter, I hope it's transformative for you. I believe wholeheartedly that integrating a manifestation approach to sales goals can revolutionize how you will achieve success.

Drawing on historical and contemporary examples, such as the manifestation techniques seen in real estate and retail apparel, we can see the benefits of this approach. Sales strategies, like breaking goals into bite-sized increments or focusing on daily targets, help in creating actionable steps toward achieving larger objectives.

To implement these techniques effectively:

- **Identify your "Magic Number".** Define a daily or weekly target that aligns with your sales goals.
- **Visualize success.** Create a clear mental image of achieving this number, incorporating specific details to reinforce motivation.
- **Stay consistent.** Engage in daily visualization and goal-setting practices to build momentum.
- **Have regular reviews.** Conduct bi-monthly assessments with a trusted partner to track progress and make necessary adjustments.

By harnessing the power of manifestation, you not only enhance your sales strategies but also transform your approach to achieving your goals, ultimately leading to greater success and fulfillment in your professional journey.

FINAL REMARKS

Own it, Live it. Take back control of your time and redefine business growth.

I challenge you to reflect on what resonated most with you in this book. Choose one strategy or idea and commit to implementing it in the next week. Start small, but aim big, and let this be the catalyst for redefining your business approach.

You now have the groundwork for a strong brand—by identifying clear target audiences, creating compelling UVPs, and mastering the art of brand strategy. You've unlocked the potential for effective business development with targeted marketing and client engagement, helping you foster stronger relationships.

You've also sharpened the "human elements" of your approach! With a clear understanding of buyer psychology, emotional intelligence, and top-notch follow-up and time-management skills, you're equipped to rise above procrastination and branding fears. You're now prepared to maintain a healthy work-life balance and incorporate manifestation selling as a powerful method to achieve your goals. What's your magic number?

By blending branding, targeted marketing, human elements, and technology, you can achieve success with less stress. This

Final Remarks

book is not just about strategies and techniques; it's about shifting your perspective on sales. See it as an opportunity to make real connections, inspire others, and grow—both personally and professionally.

As you apply these insights to your journey, remember success comes from having sound strategies, understanding people, and staying positive. You have the tools and knowledge to turn obstacles into opportunities. Now it's time to put these insights into action. Every strategy in this book empowers you to go beyond making sales—to build relationships, inspire trust, and create lasting value for your clients. The key to thriving in any business is to align your brand with your vision and build on genuine connections.

As you continue this journey, remember success isn't just about making deals—it's about making a difference. Lead with authenticity, listen deeply, and the value you create will follow. After all, a business built on genuine relationships stands the test of time.

Thank you for being part of this journey with me. May you keep growing, finding happiness, and achieving more success.

Love,
Alison
info@repmethods.com

INDEX

A
accountability, 164, 258, 285, 288
account management, 162, 176, 293
account manager, 162, 284
achieving daily sales objectives, 281
achieving limbic resonance, 218
Achieving Sales Goals, 299
achieving success in sales, 222
achieving work-life balance, 237
action strategy for sales, 82
active listening, 3, 182, 185, 188, 195, 202, 205, 211, 222, 293, 297
activities, prioritizing self-care, 238
Acuity, 134, 239, 293
Adobe Express, 42, 52, 293
advertising budgets, 119, 139, 293
advertising dollars, 103–4, 107, 113, 293
advertising expenditures, 103, 293
advertising plan, free, 145
advocacy, 77, 217
AI-powered analytics tools, 170, 293
algorithms, 35, 215
American consumerism, 27
analytics, 55, 68, 75, 128, 175
Annie McKee's work, 184
Annual revenue/time expenditure in hours, 100
Antolini, 27–28

appeal, 38–39, 130, 192, 214, 216–17
app.getmunch.com, 158, 167
appointments
  personalized, 270
  set one-on-one, 110
Appointment Scheduling, 246–47
appointment systems, 239
approach cross-merchandising, 144, 293
AR (augmented reality), 173, 293
Artificial Intelligence, 7, 293
aspirational, 26, 33, 53–54, 215
attendees, 70, 110, 134, 136–37
attention, undivided, 182, 184
automate, 163, 165–66, 263
avatar technology, 60, 64

B
B2B, 124
B2C, 125
BBC Online, 51
Becky Helmsley, 293
Best Mass Texting Services, 166
Bill Soroka, 1, 293
Bingo, 272
body language, 109, 179, 183, 189–92, 196, 205, 210, 293
boundaries, 228–30, 293
Bowling, Lauren, 100
Boyatzis, Richard E., 184
brand, luxury, 25, 40
Brand Architecture, 49–50, 75, 293
brand coach, 14, 18, 293

293

Index

brand collaborator, 65, 293
brand communities, 147, 293
brand concepts, 16, 293
brand development, 76, 108, 293
brand equity, 13, 293
brand growth, 46, 293
brand handbook, 34, 293
brand identity, 38, 43, 144, 293
branding design, 37, 293
branding elements, 38
branding strategy, 38, 44, 46, 153, 293
brand playbook, 29, 293
brand resilience, 76, 293
brand strategy, 12, 15, 17, 23, 25, 31, 42, 104, 161, 291, 293
brand visuals, 66, 293
brand voice, 33, 75, 293
Buchner, Sarah, 170
budgets, advertising sales, 119, 298
building bonds, 49, 294
building relationships, 122, 170, 191, 294
building trust, 2, 62, 138, 146, 183, 212–13, 266, 294, 299
Burton, Tara, 276
business
  coaching, 53
  mentor, 32
  service-based, 125, 140
business development by refining sales techniques, 77
business development plan, strategic, 140
business development research and outreach, 287
business development targets, 82, 111
business engagement, 122, 294
business goals, 38, 151, 245, 250, 271, 294
business growth, redefine, 291, 303
business growth areas, 146, 294

business plan, 18, 41, 125, 207, 277, 294
Business Tech Weekly, 229, 294
business-to-business, 134, 294
business-to-consumer, 113, 135, 294
buyer psychology, 180, 205, 207, 223, 291, 294

C

calendar, 162, 166, 250, 267–69, 294
CalendarBridge, 166, 294
Calendar Planning, 248
calendly.com/app/login, 166, 294
Canva, 42, 61, 101, 158, 294
Canva and Deep Reel, 61, 294
Carnegie, Dale, 155
Carrey, Jim, 278, 298
chameleoning, 189, 196, 209, 294
channels, 52–53, 58, 65, 69, 99, 294
  preferred social media, 119
charts, pie, 113–14
ChatGPT, 7, 87, 158, 294
clear prioritization strategy, 245, 294
client engagement, 47, 54, 74, 291, 294, 298
Client Engagement Checklist, 75, 294
client outreach, 240, 294
client referrals, 142, 294
client relationships, long-term, 183, 189
Closing Call-to-Action, 65, 294
closing cues, 202, 294
cognitive biases, 201, 295
Cold Calling/Lead Development, 246–47
Color Marketing Group, 40, 295
color trends, 40
communication, personalized, 117, 162
communication goals, 32, 295

communication strategy, 14, 23, 25–26, 29, 31, 33, 50, 59, 295
community engagement, 32, 51, 199, 295
community listening, 55, 295
community outreach, 240, 295
Constant Contact, 131, 166–67, 295
construction, 140, 170, 173, 214
construction materials, 85, 175, 200, 256
consumer journey, 218, 295
conversation starters, 131, 295
conversion stage, 199, 201–2
Create a vision board, 277
Create distribution lists, 129, 132
Create Reward Systems, 74
Creating Customized Experiences, 183, 196
creating opportunities for sales and referrals, 121, 295
Creating Urgency, 203
creativity, 44, 131, 234, 255, 285
CRM, 90, 151, 159–60, 162–63, 246–47, 254–55
CRM systems, 148, 153, 159, 161, 163, 259, 267, 270
cross-merchandise, 138, 295
cross-merchandising, 139, 145
Cuddy, Amy, 190
customer categories, 85, 87, 295
customer-centric approach, 54–55, 295
customer communication, 56, 295
customer emotions, 265, 296
customer engagement, 122, 154, 296, 301
customer expectations, 241, 270, 296
customer experience, 175, 264, 296
customer feedback, 55, 69–70, 75, 296
customer interactions, 11, 163, 172, 175, 184

Customer Loyalty Ideas, 124, 296
customer loyalty programs, 122–23, 296
Customer Relationship, 1, 66, 153, 296
customers
  everyday winning, 72
  loyal, 63, 125
Customer's Attention, 54
customer service, 56, 264, 296
customer service business, 112, 296
customized project orders, 239, 296

D
daily visualization, 289, 296
data, entering, 160, 164, 246–47
data analytics tools, 260, 296
data collection, 69, 296
data entry, 248, 251, 296
data management, 165, 296
decisions, informed, 55–56, 162, 173, 211, 260, 265
decision stage, 221, 296
decision tree, 208, 273, 296
Deep Reel, 59, 61–62, 64, 294, 296
Deep Reel Avatars, 60–62, 64–65
delegate, 154–55, 261, 296
demographics, 31, 85, 94, 96, 114, 169, 296
designers, 27–28, 43, 71, 112, 116, 140, 238, 287
Developing a Visual Identity, 37
Developing Intuition, 101
diagram method, 100
diagrams
  blank target market, 85
  octopus, 82, 89, 118
  primary, 114
digital calendars, 263, 296
Digital note-taking, 262
discounts, 57, 74, 124–25, 137, 296
  promotional, 35
  volume, 124

Index

discounts on goods and services, 125
distribution channels, selective, 143
distribution lists, 296
documents, 170, 258–59, 262
Doodle, 269
Dug, 84

E

EI. *See* Emotional Intelligence
email marketing, 130, 296
Email Marketing Statistics, 126
emails, personalized, 126, 129
Emotional Intelligence (EI), 109, 179–84, 188–89, 205, 208, 218, 220, 265, 291, 296–97, 300
empathy, 3, 179, 182–83, 189, 204–5, 209, 222, 265, 297
entrepreneurs and branding, 217, 297
entrepreneurship, 17, 51, 279
Establish Monitoring Tools & Data Collection, 66
event planning checklist, 73
events
 in-person, 74–75, 102, 104, 107
 personalized, 69, 135–36
exercises, target marketing diagram, 104, 303
expertise, 115, 151, 188–89, 211, 297

F

Facebook, 117, 269, 297
fear, 6, 107, 143, 185, 211, 213, 218
feedback, harness, 137
feedback for continuous improvement, 135
feedback forms, 58, 66, 134
Final Thoughts, 64
finding balance, 235
finding happiness, 292
finding solutions, 54
finding success, 226
finding support, 152
finding time, 234
focus groups, 69, 297
focus on active listening, 211, 297
follow-ups
 scheduling email, 267
 streamlined, 153
Forbes Advisor, 126, 166, 297
Forbes Magazine, 191, 297
forecasting, 149, 175–76, 255
Foundational Brand Elements, 11, 297
Foundations for branding, 12, 297
fun, 59, 70, 91, 252, 258, 271, 275, 283

G

games, 29, 50, 154, 214, 235, 271, 273
Gamma.app, 158, 297
Generation Alpha, 216
Gmail, 165–66, 268, 297
GMass, 166, 297
goal manifestation, 279, 297, 301
 use sales, 242
goal refinements, 288, 297
goals
 clear, 198, 200–202, 302
 strategic, 176, 198
goal-setting practices, 289, 297
Goal Visualization, 277, 297
Goleman, Daniel, 184
Grassi Pietre, 95, 128, 297, 307
growth, 146, 263, 297

H

happiness, 26, 277
Harvard Business Review, 230–31, 249, 297
Harvard Business School Press, 184, 297
Harvard Medical School, 57, 297
hashtags, 36, 53, 55, 297
health, mental, 218, 227–28, 237, 277
Health Centre NZ, 230, 297

help consumers, 109
help individuals, 260
Hemsley, 297
High brand equity, 13, 297
hiring individuals, 215
homeowners, 113, 230
Hootsuite, 168, 297
hosting, 70, 72, 102–3, 146
hosting events, 135
Hosting events and workshops, 69
hourly rate, current, 101
human-centric approach, 183, 205
human element, 2, 50, 179–82, 184, 188, 190, 207, 226, 291
human element in sales, 2, 188, 226
Humanizing Tasks, 243

I
if you build it, 15
increments, bite-sized, 288
Indirect Selling Technique, 9, 297
industry groups, 85, 124, 132, 186, 260
Influence of Visuals in Branding, 37, 297
influencers, 215–16
innovation, 28, 44, 64, 116, 158, 170, 173, 177, 233, 297
insecurities, 212–13
instincts, 179, 253
 consumer purchase, 208
 gut, 217
 natural, 253
integration, 61, 163, 177, 260–61
interactions
 human, 150, 182, 184, 205
 in-person, 99
 personalized, 51, 133
 social, 214
intuition, 101, 107, 161, 205, 207–8, 222, 251, 255, 298
inventory, 285
 keeping, 226
 new, 285
Inventory Check & Update, 248
inventory management, merchandising strategies, 159
investment, 69, 102, 152, 164, 176–77, 197, 204
invitations, 71, 130
invoices, creating, 240
invoicing, 163, 176

J
job, salesperson's, 220
journey
 buyer's, 221
 psychological sales, 218
journeys
 entrepreneurial, 151, 165
 selling, 218, 302

K
Kappel, Mike, 54
key demographics, 18
key money makers, 103
key networking groups, 107
key performance indicators. *See* KPIs
keystone markup, 283, 298
kitchen, 16, 70, 110, 112–13, 115, 117, 140, 143, 173, 218
Koch, Richard, 93
KPIs (key performance indicators), 149, 176, 298

L
language, 41, 190, 203, 298
Latham, Shannon, 89
Laura Mae Martin, 249, 298
law of attraction, 277, 282, 298
lead-generation opportunities, 55, 298
light bulb, 130, 141, 246, 298
limbic resonance, 182–84, 189
LinkedIn, 35, 58, 117, 298
logo, 16, 24, 38–39, 41–42, 75, 298
Low-Hanging Fruit, 92, 111, 298
Loyalty Program Development, 298

Index

Loyalty Program Ideas, 125
loyalty rewards, 270, 298

M

magic number, 283, 287, 289, 291, 298
Make Order Makers, 18, 60, 82, 209, 298, 307
Managing Marketing Time and Resources, 99
Manifestation History, 276
Manifestation in Sales, 279
manifestation selling, 275–76
manifestation techniques, 277, 282, 288
marketing and branding, 153, 298
marketing and sales strategies, 114, 298
MarketingCharts, 127
Marketing-drive.com, 52
marketing efforts, 77, 99, 161–62, 295, 298
marketing emails, 129, 261, 298
marketing game, 65, 298
marketing plans, 161, 166–67, 299
marketing service agencies, 167, 299
marketing strategy, 44, 82, 115, 299
marketing subcontractor, 50, 299
MarketSpotAudit, 210
mass marketing strategies, 166, 299
mindfulness, 226–28, 230–31, 233, 299
mindfulness and meditation, 226, 230, 299

N

National Kitchen & Bath Association, 44, 299
Navigating Challenges, 76, 299
negativity, 40, 299
negotiation, 113, 299
network, 17, 50, 83, 89, 117, 133, 143, 228

networking, 76, 96, 102–4, 111, 135, 247–48, 285, 299
networking groups, 6, 119, 133, 254, 299
New strategies, 211, 213–14, 216–17, 299
New York Times, 276
New York Times Wirecutter, 215, 299
Nielsen Norman Group, 128, 131, 299
Nipane, Anita, 39
NotaryCoach.com, 1, 299
number, manifestation sales, 287

O

objections, 183, 189, 204, 299
office dynamics, 299
office hours, 252, 299
office time, 253
Old strategies, 211–12, 214–15, 217, 300
Olesen, Jacob, 40
online engagement, 104, 300
online events, 73, 167, 300
OpenAI, 7, 158, 167, 300
Order Takers, 2, 18–19, 60, 63, 82, 84, 209, 220, 243, 307
organization, 19, 71, 82, 95, 176, 178, 180, 248, 262–63
otter.ai, 172, 262, 300
Outlook's drag-and-drop system, 268
outsourcing, 101, 151–52
Oxford Languages, 276, 300

P

parallel demographics, 87, 300
Pareto principle, 93, 101, 115, 244–45, 248, 300
partnerships, 122, 133, 138, 140, 143–45, 300–301
peers, 135, 137
Penttinen, Valeria, 52
perception, 230, 245, 300

performance, 53, 55, 260, 271, 287–88
persona and UVP, 18, 300
personalization, 64, 126, 138, 162, 269, 300
personalize customer interactions, 69
Personalized outreach, 122, 126
personalize marketing efforts, 74, 300
personal time, 228, 231, 300
phone calls, 57, 122, 130–31, 163, 197, 199–200, 229, 246–47, 250, 282, 300
phone conversations, 130, 300
physical activities, 226, 235, 238, 300
pillar elements, 18
pipeline, 280, 300
  infallible, 180, 276, 281
PK (product knowledge), 110, 189, 287, 300
planning, strategic, 149–50
Porch Group Media, 126, 300
positivity, 279, 282
POS systems, 161, 282, 300
Power of Color in Marketing, 39, 300
Power of Emotional Intelligence, 184, 300
power of storytelling, 45, 300
power of storytelling in branding, 45, 300
power of vision and storytelling, 28, 301
power of vision and storytelling in branding, 28, 301
precious time, 99–100, 196, 239
predictive analytics, 171–72, 175
prioritization chart, 118
prioritization octopus, 113
prioritizing accounts, 245
problem-solving, 202, 301
procrastination, 241–42, 291
productivity, 157, 171, 180, 227, 237, 249, 301

product knowledge. *See* PK
professional development strategies, 146, 301, 303
Professional marketers, 15, 29
programs
  industry mentorship, 188
  logo-generating software, 42
  mapping, 253
  twelve-step, 148, 196
project management software, 259, 301
project management tools, 258, 301
psychological approach, 199, 301
psychology, 3, 5, 63, 205, 277, 301
purchase
  new home, 191
  past, 198, 281
Purchasing Power, 191, 301

Q

quarry, 27–28
questionnaires, creating tailored, 134
questions
  answer, 6, 169, 250
  asking, 185
  open-ended, 137
  time efficiency, 91
Quora, 58, 301

R

races, 15, 90, 274
ranking, 91, 94, 119, 166, 246–47
rates, closure, 171–72
reactive salesperson, 84
reactivity, 195
real estate agents, 213, 282
Rebate program, 124
Recognizing Closing Signals, 202, 301
referrals, 50, 77, 110, 121, 141, 146, 177, 211, 222, 264, 295, 300
relationships, long-term, 122, 145–46, 182, 202

Index

Rep Methods, 19–20, 39–40, 50, 65, 128, 155, 307
responses
 automated, 57
 automating email, 259
 scripted, 266
responsiveness, 56, 66, 152, 177, 301
Rethink Business Relationships, 301
RethinkBusiness Relationships & Attraction Selling, 121
revenue, 83, 90–92, 100, 103, 111, 113, 138, 177, 245
Reviews and feedback, 66, 301
ROI, 152, 177
RSVP execution plan, 71, 301
RSVP lists, 71, 110

S

sales associates, underperforming, 84
sales calls, 117, 257, 283, 287, 301
sales data, historical, 165, 172
sales history data, 85, 301
sales intuition, 101, 165, 302
sales process, 76, 172, 182–84, 188, 202, 205, 264, 302
sales strategies, 6, 82–83, 89, 97, 114, 161, 205, 288–89, 298, 302
sales superstars, 210, 302
sales techniques, 70, 211, 264, 286, 302
SEO strategies, 261
small business owners, 5, 52, 65, 100, 157, 167, 171, 226, 281
Social Media Creative, 247, 302
social media listening, 56, 137, 302
social media management, 150, 302
social media monitoring, 69, 302
social media platforms, 52, 99, 302
social media posts, 255, 277, 302

social media scheduling tools, 259, 302
squirrel mentality, 84, 302
streamline operations, 161, 178, 302
stress management, 230, 233, 303
Strong Brand Social, 29, 303

T

target marketing, 5–6, 11, 15, 99, 112, 114, 148, 150, 254
Target Marketing & Prioritization Table, 94, 303
target marketing list, 115, 303
target marketing organization process, 90, 303
target marketing plan, 6, 303
target marketing tactics, 293, 303
target marketing technique, 198, 303
target markets, 14–15, 25, 56, 95, 103, 145, 171, 303
target persona and UVP, 47, 58, 75, 102
target persona andUVP, 20
target persona story, 32
target personas to shift, 161
Texas, 130, 159, 197
TextRequest, 132
thirty-day calendar, 252–53, 303
TikTok, 35, 51–52, 54, 117, 214, 216, 303
time blocking, 227, 255–56
Time Blocking and Sales, 255
time blocks, 95, 240
time management, 19, 99, 111, 130, 165, 180, 227, 240, 244, 250, 252, 255, 263
time-management skills, 243, 291, 303
time-management strategies, 83, 227, 303
Todoist, 259, 303
training and professional development strategies, 146

training programs, 148, 303
training salespeople, 85, 303
Trunk Tools, 170, 303
Trustpilot, 66, 134, 303

U
unique value proposition. *See* UVP
Unlocking Business Development, 79, 304
Use of Avatars in Marketing, 60
USPS, 57
UVP (unique value proposition), 11–13, 17–19, 25, 29, 32–33, 35, 38, 41, 47, 50, 53, 58, 65, 75–76, 102, 118, 291, 300, 304
UVP & Target Persona, 12, 23, 304
UVP statements, 17, 33, 220, 304

V
Validating Goals, 203, 304
videography, 62, 214, 304
video testimonials, 67, 214, 216, 304
virtual assistants, 168, 171
Virtual reality, 173
visual branding process, 39, 304
visual identity, 14, 37–38, 44, 46–47, 304
Visuals in Branding, 37, 297
Volunteer Work, 247
VR, 173, 176

W
Walsh-McGrath, Elaine, 58
Washington, 229
Washingtonians, 230
WhatsApp, 269, 304
WIFI, 73, 254, 304
Wight, Katie, 29
women, 73, 154, 188, 191, 213, 279, 304
woo-woo, 277, 288, 304
work environment, 239, 304
work-life balance, 180, 223, 225–26, 235, 300

Work-Life Balance Conversation, 225, 304
workshops, 20, 69–70, 136, 141, 150, 155, 238, 304, 307
sales training, 159, 180
work smarter, 5
Wunderlist, 260, 304

X
Xennial, 168, 304

Y
Yahoo, 165, 169, 268, 304
yoga, 232, 304
YouTube, 54, 218, 233, 304

Z
zip codes, 15, 304
Zoho, 168, 259, 304
Zoom, 304

GIFT

Thanks for reading this book, scan the QR Code below with your phone and claim your free 1:1 coaching session ASAP!

CONTACT US

Participated in one of our events? Let me know you were there!

ABOUT THE AUTHOR

Alison Mullins owns Rep Methods LLC and is a highly influential figure in the construction materials industry. Alison is known for her exceptional expertise around natural stone and extensive global experiences working within this conglomerate industry. Her influence is particularly notable in the sales and procurement of materials for clients and projects, which brought her to write her first and bestselling book: *The Art of Selling, We Make Order Makers, Not Order Takers*.

Alison is still selling! She helps with business development and sales for Grassi Pietre SRL of Vicenza, Italy. Grassi Pietre is a vertical manufacturer of natural limestone in the Veneto Region. www.grassipietre.it

With over 25 years of sales experience, Rep Methods offers coaching, workshops, and seminars. www.repmethods.com

www.ingramcontent.com/pod-product-compliance
Lightning Source LLC
Chambersburg PA
CBHW070937230426
43666CB00011B/2466